PRAISE FOR *FATAL ATTRACTION*

"The perfection of Leonard's volume a.
manifest to me not only in its wonderfully detailed anaiyses, ...
the many moments that I found myself seamlessly entering into a
discussion with them. It's difficult to imagine a student who would
not respond with enthusiasm to this cleanly and accessibly written,
engaging, knowledgeable book about the film that inaugurated the
genre of the "erotic thriller," and very easy to imagine it as a pleasure
for interested cinephiles with a glass of wine within reach and a free
evening or two."

Martha P. Nochimson, author of Dying to Belong:
Gangster Movies in Hollywood and Hong Kong, *and*
The Passion of David Lynch: Wild at Heart in Hollywood

Wiley-Blackwell Studies in Film and Television

Experienced media studies teachers know that real breakthroughs in the classroom are often triggered by texts that an austere notion of the canon would disqualify. Unlike other short book series, *Wiley-Blackwell Studies in Film and Television* works from a broad field of prospective film and television programs, selected less for their adherence to definitions of "art" than for their resonance with audiences.

From *Top Hat* to *Hairspray*, from early sitcoms to contemporary forensic dramas, the series encompasses a range of film and television material that reflects diverse genres, forms, styles and periods. The texts explored here are known and recognized world-wide for their ability to generate discussion and debate about evolving media industries as well as, crucially, representations and conceptualizations of gender, class, citizenship, race, consumerism and capitalism, and other facets of identity and experience. *This series* is designed to communicate these themes clearly and effectively to media studies students at all levels while also introducing groundbreaking scholarship of the very highest caliber. These are the films and shows we really want to watch, the new 'teachable canon' of alternative classics that range from silent film to *CSI*.

FATAL ATTRACTION
SUZANNE LEONARD

⊗**WILEY-BLACKWELL**

A John Wiley & Sons, Ltd., Publication

This edition first published 2009
© 2009 Suzanne Leonard

Blackwell Publishing was acquired by John Wiley & Sons in February 2007. Blackwell's publishing program has been merged with Wiley's global Scientific, Technical, and Medical business to form Wiley-Blackwell.

Registered Office
John Wiley & Sons Ltd, The Atrium, Southern Gate, Chichester, West Sussex, PO19 8SQ, United Kingdom

Editorial Offices
350 Main Street, Malden, MA 02148-5020, USA
9600 Garsington Road, Oxford, OX4 2DQ, UK
The Atrium, Southern Gate, Chichester, West Sussex, PO19 8SQ, UK

For details of our global editorial offices, for customer services, and for information about how to apply for permission to reuse the copyright material in this book please see our website at www.wiley.com/wiley-blackwell.

The right of Suzanne Leonard to be identified as the author of this work has been asserted in accordance with the Copyright, Designs and Patents Act 1988.

Wiley also publishes its books in a variety of electronic formats. Some content that appears in print may not be available in electronic books.

Designations used by companies to distinguish their products are often claimed as trademarks. All brand names and product names used in this book are trade names, service marks, trademarks or registered trademarks of their respective owners. The publisher is not associated with any product or vendor mentioned in this book. This publication is designed to provide accurate and authoritative information in regard to the subject matter covered. It is sold on the understanding that the publisher is not engaged in rendering professional services. If professional advice or other expert assistance is required, the services of a competent professional should be sought.

Library of Congress Cataloging-in-Publication Data

Leonard, Suzanne.
Fatal attraction / Suzanne Leonard.
    p. cm.
Includes bibliographical references and index.
ISBN 978-1-4051-7376-6 (hardcover: alk. paper) – ISBN 978-1-4051-7375-9 (pbk.: alk. paper)
1. Fatal attraction (Motion picture) I. Title.
PN1997.F348L46 2009
070.4′4–dc22

                                                            2008041560

A catalogue record for this book is available from the British Library.

Set in 10.5/13pt Minion by SPi Publisher Services, Pondicherry, India
Printed and bound in Malaysia by Vivar Printing Sdn Bhd

001   2009

Contents

List of Illustrations   vi
Acknowledgments   vii

Introduction   1

1. "I'm Not Going to be *Ignored*, Dan":
    Narrative Cues for Suspense and Intimidation   6

2. American Genres in *Fatal Attraction*   34

3. Career Women of the 1980s:
    Feminism and the Reception History of *Fatal Attraction*   62

4. Erotic Sexuality, AIDS, and the Case for Staying Faithful   87

5. Female Identities and Postfeminist Paradigms   108

Notes   121
Works Cited   129
Index   135

List of Illustrations

Alex sitting in Dan's office   11

Alex sitting surrounded by cartons of junk   17

Close-up of the phone   20

Boiled bunny crosscutting sequence   25

Close-up of running water   31

Alex sitting alone on opera night   38

Dan looking out the window   43

Alex comes to the condo   68

Alex committing suicide   84

Dan and Alex making love   90

Alex attacking Dan   91

Bridget Jones watching *Fatal Attraction*   109

Alex with a butcher knife   111

Alex's death   119

Acknowledgments

This book owes its greatest debt to the skilled attention of series editors Diane Negra and Yvonne Tasker, whose careful readings and theoretical rigor have underpinned this project. I especially want to recognize Diane's professional generosity, which I have benefited from for over many years. I thank Wiley-Blackwell editor Jayne Fargnoli for our many lively discussions, all of which made the process of writing this book a pure pleasure. Margot Morse skillfully handled the book's production details.

Deepest appreciation goes to my colleagues at Simmons College, especially Kelly Hager, who read some of the earliest drafts of this work with wonderful care. As well, I thank Simmons faculty members Lowry Pei, Cathie Mercier, Sarah Leonard, Pamela Bromberg, Renée Bergland, Douglas Perry, Sheldon George, Afaa Michael Weaver, David Gullette, Richard Wollman, Anna Sandoval and Vonda Powell. I also want to thank Emily Fox Kales for helping me decipher some of *Fatal Attraction*'s trickier details. I continue to appreciate the advising I received as a doctoral student at the University of Wisconsin-Milwaukee, and want to recognize especially the guidance of Gregory Jay, Jane Gallop, and Vicki Callahan.

The fact that this book is able to survey the extensive press surrounding *Fatal Attraction* reflects the meticulous research skills of my project assistant Allison Lakomski. The process of interpreting the film has been aided by the terrific insights of my students at Simmons, especially those who took The Art of Film in the Fall of 2006 and 2007. I thank them all for their enthusiasm. I would also like to recognize the Simmons College Fund for Research as well as the Gender and Cultural Studies program at Simmons, both of which enabled necessary research for this project.

Finally, I dedicate this book to my family, Donald, Anne, and Keith Leonard, in thanks for their love, support, and perpetual good humor.

Introduction

Since its widely touted release in 1987, *Fatal Attraction*'s signature mix of sexuality, thrills, fear, and family values has proved a lucrative, if controversial, entry into the annals of American cinema. The film grossed over $156 million in domestic profits, was nominated for six Oscars, and incongruously made more money at the box office during its second week than its first, a factoid that confirms the zeal of audiences whose word of mouth campaign fueled the film's skyrocketing success. The film played in American theaters for an astonishing 39 weeks, many of them accompanied by shrieks of "Kill the bitch!" which arose from impassioned audiences. Appreciated as a keenly effective deterrent to infidelity, a movie ticket was perhaps seen as an economical substitute for years of expensive marital therapy. The film also indulged the interests of the prurient: sex scenes in *Fatal Attraction* are as violent as they are graphic, and the film demonstrated an almost gleeful willingness to mock propriety and restraint in favor of the sensationalized and the exploitative. One need look no farther for confirmation of this ethos than to the film's most iconic image, a moment forever memorialized in the term "bunny boiler."

Fatal Attraction's exposé of a man who embarks on a casual affair which later reveals itself to have disastrous consequences also had deep resonance in its historical moment, and *Fatal Attraction* quickly became understood as a zeitgeist film for its skillful treatment of cultural anxieties regarding career women, sexuality, employment, and infidelity. At a time when "family values" were gaining national currency, Dan Gallagher's (Michael Douglas) apparently unpremeditated affair was seen by many to illustrate the dangerous consequences of illicit sexuality, eventualities which for Dan included an unwanted pregnancy, alienation from his family, and threats to his life and those of his loved ones. Such consequences were also thought to gesture to other related cultural epidemics, most obviously, the burgeoning AIDS crisis. In short, if the sociopolitical rhetoric of the Reagan era imbued marital fidelity with attributions which extended far beyond the domestic, Dan's selfish act was touted as a threat to the institution of the family as a whole, the bedrock upon which the nation was thought to rest. The film's morality tale was indeed hard to miss.

Fatal Attraction also generated interest for what were seen as its charged gender politics; thanks to its timing and treatment of Alex Forrest (Glenn Close) as a career woman who refuses to relinquish Dan after their one weekend together, the film was widely taken as a comment on the failures of the second-wave feminist movement. In turn, it carried the dubious distinction of being one of the first cultural products to be publicly named as part of the feminist "backlash." The film's insistence on the unforeseen perils of female liberation incited considerable rancor, especially amongst feminists who found its portrayals offensive to women. One anecdote will prove instructive: shortly after the film's release, *Village Voice* critic Amy Taubin described a conversation she had with Laura Mulvey, whose "Visual Pleasure and Narrative Cinema" is considered perhaps the seminal essay of feminist film theory. A crestfallen Taubin was trying to explain to Mulvey why *Fatal Attraction* made her feel so awful, and Mulvey, not knowing Adrian Lyne was the director of the film, told Taubin that that the only film that had ever made *her* feel that bad was *9½ Weeks* (1986), another Lyne vehicle. As Taubin explains, "In Lyne's world a woman's sense of self is totally a function of her value in men's eyes" (1987: 90). *Fatal Attraction*'s ability to penetrate the psyche of even the most skilled female watchers confirms the extratextual impact of the film; in short, audiences greeted *Fatal Attraction* with the realization that meaningful attributions of gender and sexuality were publically at stake.

As the controversy over the film crested, the conversation turned increasingly on the issue of *Fatal Attraction*'s pitting of a maniacal career woman against a sympathetic nuclear family, and the family's triumphant albeit murderous victory in turn affirmed the worth of "traditional" values. Alex came to designate not only a psychotic stalker, but also the quintessential "desperate woman" whose career aspirations have precluded her marital success and left her envying the connubial pleasures to be found in the domestic sphere. In this way, the film put feminism's past and future in the national spotlight, thanks especially to the fact that it situated decisions over marriage, reproduction, and employment as vexed questions for all women. Though the lasting implications of this discussion were not wholly clear in the late 1980s, in fact the film demonstrated an uncanny ability to cleave women, and, more broadly, to diagnose competing cultural investments in notions of "work" and "family." Such distinctions proved prescient, as this divide would become, in the years following the film's release, highly paradigmatic of the postfeminist era.

The film's rather meteoric rise to popularity in 1987 continues to guarantee, in fact, its iconic status in the past and present landscape of American media culture. The film is credited with, amongst other achievements, having inaugurated a new film genre, the "erotic thriller," which is so named for having given equal consideration to sex and to violence, as well as offering opportunity and rationalization for their considerable comingling. As an origin text, *Fatal Attraction* is repeatedly quoted, referenced, and parodied in other venues, and the term "bunny boiler" has entered the popular lexicon both to bespeak Alex's penchant for inventive means of revenge, and as a shorthand for women willing to resort to sadistic methods with which to make their presence known to current or former lovers. While the bunny boiler image has been referenced ad nauseam in popular culture, its most lasting attribution is as a rejoinder against making poor romantic decisions, and especially, as a caution for men against fraternizing with an intense woman, lest attraction and exciting sex blind one to her sinister potentialities. *Fatal Attraction* continues to stand as the cautionary tale par excellence, one whose chilling effects on the male libido remain legendary. In *Sleepless in Seattle* (1993), Sam Baldwin (Tom Hanks) tells his son, "Well I saw it and it scared the shit out of me. It scared the shit out of every man in

America!" As if to underscore this statement, *Fatal Attraction*'s 20th-year anniversary in December 2007 was celebrated with an AP wire story that quoted Glenn Close saying, "That movie struck a very, very, raw nerve. Feminists hated the movie and that was shocking to me ... But now Alex is considered a heroine. Men still come up to me and say, 'You scared the ... outta me,' Sometimes they say 'you saved my marriage'" (*Hartford Courant*, 2007: D2). Close either intentionally or inadvertently quotes *Sleepless in Seattle*, in effect producing a discursive hall of mirrors which confirms Alex's status as a figure traded back and forth between actual people and fictionalized representations. In this, Alex Forrest lives as a spectral figure in both real and imagined worlds, realms that mutually influence each other. That Alex's image can still shame men into fidelity also illustrates the extent to which *Fatal Attraction* has lodged itself in the national consciousness as championing marital success and stability, and the film often serves as a cultural barometer as spectators past and present measure their relationships against its specter. Even today, online fan sites rehash Dan's culpability, offer justifications for Alex's reactions, and squabble over questions of sexual fidelity.

The purpose of this volume is to acknowledge this complicated history, parsing out why *Fatal Attraction* is and continues to be a fixture on the American cinematic landscape. Moving from an analysis of the film's formal features and key motifs (Chapter One), to its status as a hybrid genre piece (Chapter Two), the volume arrives at cultural considerations in its final three chapters. Taking up, alternatively, the feminist debate surrounding the film in the 1980s (Chapter Three), issues of sexuality and adultery (Chapter Four), and the lasting impact of the film on postfeminism (Chapter Five), the volume affords *Fatal Attraction* consideration as a film whose interjection into the reigning social debates of its time succeeded in framing the terms by which cultural and especially feminist issues have been understood for years hence. Perhaps this is due to the fact that *Fatal Attraction* forces American culture to confront some of the most profound questions of modern life – it asks audiences to ponder what constitutes an immoral act, to reconsider what responsibilities and obligations they owe their families, to weigh sometimes competing needs for security and adventure, and to examine how relationships between sexuality, intimacy, and partnership are imagined and then enforced. *Fatal Attraction*'s status as a bunny boiler ensures that it will forever be associated with a maniacal act of revenge and retribution, yet this volume aims to minimize that designation in favor of examining the more complicated commentary the film has engendered on sexuality, morality, marriage, and relational responsibility. While the book examines and appreciates the singular moments of terror or pleasure for which the film is most famous, it nevertheless privileges discussion of the film as a cultural object, one that has made lasting interventions into considerations of the ways we lead our lives.

"I'm Not Going to be *Ignored*, Dan":
Narrative Cues for Suspense and Intimidation

A list of the sights and sounds that anchor *Fatal Attraction* would likely include the following: A phone that suddenly rings, interrupting a dinner party. The sight of a couple enjoying a dinner of pasta and red wine, chatting over the mellifluous tones of *Madame Butterfly*. The sound of a boiling teakettle, emitting its high-pitched tone. An image of a woman and child, strolling through a suburban amusement park on a windy day. Taken out of context, none of these selections sound ominous, yet in *Fatal Attraction* each becomes a harbinger of danger, an emotional, visual, or aural evocation that a pestilence has been unleashed. The incessantly ringing telephone, for instance, intrudes jarringly and unexpectedly into the Gallagher home, a terrifying reminder of the scorned woman who uses it as a last desperate connection to the married man with whom she has become obsessed. (The telephone figures so strongly in the emotional register of *Fatal Attraction*, in fact, as to appear as the resting image in the menu for the 15th-anniversary DVD edition. Positioned next to shifting images of Michael Douglas and Glenn Close, the white phone sits against an all-white background and rings intermittently.)

The phone rings a total of ten times in the film, a number that perhaps belies the forceful sensation of disruption that accompanies each of these intrusions. Prone to phone at any time of the day or night, Alex is as likely to interrupt the Gallaghers' sleep as she is to intrude on their moving day. Cut off from all other means of communication, Alex employs the phone for a perverse objective: even if she cannot have Dan, as she intones so brilliantly, she will *not* be forgotten. Soon, even the suggestion of a ring is enough to make Dan, the guilty, harangued husband, sweat, gasp, and run for the phone. Patent is his relief when the caller is not Alex, although, like a Pavlovian casualty, Dan's reprieve is only momentary, lasting until the next caller – innocent or not.

The propensity to make the ordinary seem frightening serves as a mainstay of the horror and thriller genres, genres to which *Fatal Attraction* owes considerable allegiance. Chapter Two catalogues these various affiliations and Chapter One prepares for such a discussion by atomizing the film's chilling effects in order to unpack how they are manufactured through formal, film-specific strategies, technological components that coalesce in such a way so as to produce maximum emotional intensity. It is easy to cite, for instance, the discovery of the boiled bunny in the Gallagher family kitchen as a terrifying moment. Easier to forget, however, is that the sequence is shot and edited to emphasize the simultaneity of Ellen's (Ellen Hamilton Latzen) discovery that the bunny is gone, and Beth's (Anne Archer) vision of the bunny's lifeless body bobbing in a pot of steaming water. Unpacking the technical devices and structuring motifs that contribute to *Fatal Attraction*'s iconicity, this chapter argues that what we perceive as scary in the film has much to do with the text's ability to use cinematic devices to frame the ordinary in unconventional ways. The sequences and images to be analyzed include: white as a structuring color scheme; the phone; break-ins and the boiled bunny; and the motif of boiling water.

In Black and White

The opening shot of *Fatal Attraction* pans across a New York City skyline during an orange twilight, ventures past tall water towers and rooftops, and eventually arrives at the Gallaghers' New York apartment, a shot accompanied by sounds of the city street. As the camera closes in, Beth Gallagher appears in a window and pulls down a shade. The focus on windows and shades borrows blatantly from Hitchcock, who used the motif as a way of delineating activities and interests that disturb the family, and similar moments can be seen in both *Shadow of a Doubt* (1943) and *Rear Window* (1954). *Fatal Attraction*'s opening nevertheless most closely mimics Hitchcock's *Psycho* (1960), which traverses the skyline of Phoenix before entering the motel room of a couple having an affair. Yet while *Psycho*'s camera locates the couple by travelling through their window in a continuous shot, penetrating its interior, *Fatal Attraction* cuts after the shade is pulled down. Audiences can no longer look from afar because Beth has blocked the sightline, a move that suggests her ability (at this point) to protect her family from unwanted intrusion.

On the other side of the window, the scenes are also wholly different. In *Psycho* the camera's entry into this transient space underscores the seediness of the actions taking place within it. Outside the sanctity of a marriage, a couple meets illicitly in an impersonal hotel room, their matrimonial prospects made pessimistic when Sam (John Gavin) tells Marion (Janet Leigh) that marriage would be difficult because he is still dogged by alimony payments to his opportunistic and un-deserving ex-wife. *Fatal Attraction*'s homage to the opening of *Psycho* patently inverses this tone of marital desperation and capitulation – rather than suffering the burdens of fiscal inadequacy, the Gallaghers are clearly enjoying its bounties. Conveying a sense of comfortable abundance, the first indoor shot of the Gallaghers' condo features a space cluttered with the detritus of family life: toys are strewn about, underclothes hang in the bathroom to dry, and a dog rests lazily on the couch beside a happy child.

Palpable is the sense of familial harmony, a sensibility nicely under-scored by the family's apparel. Clothed all in white, the family appears in varying stages of undress: Dan wears a shirt without pants, as does his wife Beth, and their 5-year-old daughter Ellen sports an over-sized tee-shirt, perhaps one of her father's.[1] Yet, the family inhabits their semi-nudity casually, as if there is no need or room for embar-rassment in this domestic Eden. (Further confirmation for the uniformity of this unblemished world arrives via Ellen's babysitter who is also dressed entirely in white.) This structuring color scheme also continues after the couple returns home that same night, after Dan and Beth attend the book party at which Dan first makes Alex's acquaintance. In this nighttime scene, a white-shirted Dan is corralled into taking the family dog for a walk before he retires. By the time he returns home, hoping to join the connubial bed, a white-shirted Ellen has already usurped his place there. In one of the many scenes where the camera shares Dan's subjectivity, Dan enters the room to find both his wife and daughter happily ensconced in their white sheets. Though a mildly exasperated look appears on his face, Dan is also sweetly tolerant, and the tone again identifies the Gallaghers' home as a harmonious domestic space. While Dan wished to spend the night with his wife, the scene most likely assigns him a lonely sojourn on the couch.

Perhaps not coincidentally, white also dominates another scene of coitus interruptus. While getting ready for a dinner party they are hosting, Beth appears in soft focus in white panties and a white bra seated in front of her vanity, bathed in soft orange light. The scene aligns the gaze of the camera with Dan's sightline, since Dan sits in a white shirt on the bed, watching her sensually apply lipstick and lotion, a look of enrapt attention and desire on his face. Overcome by desire for his wife, he approaches her, kisses her from behind and pries her legs apart, as they watch themselves in the mirror. Suddenly the doorbell blares, announcing the arrival of their guests. Again, the exasperation is palpable, but the scene suggests a momentary deferral of pleasure rather than an unyielding denial of it.

Such associations between white, the pristine state of the family's consciousness, and Dan's and Beth's easy sexual rapport might seem to make room for an obvious correlation between white and family sanctity, creating an opportunity for Alex to emerge as the dark other. Yet, the film complicates this schema, for Alex too becomes relent-lessly associated with white, her frame topped off by curly blonde hair which is so light that it appears almost preternaturally white. She too has an all-white apartment, a white phone, an off-white umbrella, and she appears numerous times in white – in a white suit, in a white rain-coat, in a white robe, in a white tee-shirt, in a white negligee, and in a white scoop-necked dress. While the Gallaghers' white life is shot, however, in soft red and orange tones, Alex's in turn often appears in cool blues. When associated with Alex, the film underscores white as a stark blankness associated with a cold, lonely existence. This attribution is made most apparent in the numerous scenes set in her home, since Alex has little furniture in her cavernous loft apartment save a bed, nightstand, and dilapidated exercise bike. In this, whiteness presents a visual correlative to her apparently empty life – stark white walls, floors, and bedding mock her single state.

This presentation of Alex's apartment as playing host to little more than empty air was no doubt deliberate, and, while publicizing the film, director Adrian Lyne made a habit of repeating the factoid that in order to get a feel for how a single career woman's apartment should look, he previewed Polaroids of actual editors' apartments in New York. His remarks on what he saw in those shots did nothing to endear him to feminists, for he was particularly fond of pointing out that he found such spaces rather spartan and depressing. In one of the many reported iterations of his impressions, he notes in the director's commentary that all the women had were "piles of manuscripts by the bed; it was rather mournful."[2] When associated with Alex, white colludes with a larger visual project of recording a life that is harsh and empty, an existence she tries hard to populate (both literally and figuratively). Connoting not abundance but absence, Alex's white life has a harsh, antiseptic feel.

White is not the only schema to which Alex is assigned, however, for she appears in black frequently as well. In particular, Alex wears black when she is out in public, and especially when intruding on Dan's life in some way. She wears a black dress the first time they meet, and sports a black leather coat when she appears in his office, on the night that she follows him home to his country house, and on the day that she takes Ellen to the amusement park. A close reading of the color palette of *Fatal Attraction* thereby reveals a film whose visual meanings are contextual, and perhaps, more aptly, interrelational. While there is hardly a precise pattern to Alex's fashionable ensembles, she tends to trade in contrasts – she appears in either black or white, with heavy make-up, such as dark eyeliner and red lipstick, or without any make-up at all, as she is in the film's climactic final scene. The stark contrast between these two extremes complies with her characterization as a woman who resides only on the poles of existence: either intensely

Alex arrives uninvited for a surprise visit at Dan's office.

sexual, or intensely enraged, dramatic oppositions inform her emotional register and correlate in turn to her visual appearance. The alternation of black and white also bespeaks the film's noir-like preoccupations with good and evil, since the temptation of the dark side competes with the allure of the familiar and safe. Alex's color fluctuations code her as a figure who shape-shifts between these binaries; though she can move within the supposedly morally pure world, she threatens to contaminate it with her dark impulses.

Fatal Attraction's primary interest lies in the dynamics of a family triangulated by an intruder, and the film's color evocations speak to these psychological relations, tracing as they do the configurations between husband and wife, husband and mistress, and mistress and wife. The morning after Dan spends the night with Alex, for instance, he returns home to his apartment and wears a blue dress shirt, open at the neckline, as he sits on the phone with Beth. Talking at the other end of the line, Beth appears in a full-length blue fall coat, partially open, and both types of apparel make a deep V on their wearer's chest. As they converse, the ensembles of husband and wife visually mirror each other. Beth is not yet aware of the affair, thus this color mapping renders the marital relation as still unified and strong. Notably, we never see Alex in blue, a color that is perhaps reserved for the rightful couple. Yet, later that same day Alex aggressively and deliberately rips Dan's blue shirt, the same one he wore while on the phone with his wife.

Symbolic color configurations also organize the spectacle which occurs the night that Dan brings the bunny home to Ellen, in a vision inspired by a Norman Rockwellian aesthetic. Beth and Ellen sit on their living-room floor, dressed in white, and the family is again lit in soft, orange hues. The bunny too is white, which the film emphasizes by later revealing that Ellen has named him "Whitey." This time Dan sports a dark coat, as he has just returned home in a rental car after Alex destroyed his car by pouring acid on it, his commute accompanied by her frantic taped ravings. While the family is inside their country home, Alex stands outside the picture window looking in, wearing a black coat that strongly echoes Dan's. While Alex is spatially removed from the scene, a fact that precipitates her vomiting, Dan is perhaps not as present inside the home as he would appear. Instead, the color palette distances Dan, rendering him unable to fully participate in Beth's and Ellen's excitement and surely reflects his now panic-stricken state of mind. In a similar iteration of Dan's increasing isolation from the family, the night that Dan finally tells Beth about the affair he is dressed all in black, whereas she wears light khaki pants and a white, lightly patterned shirt. Again, the dissonance between their outfits reflects the psychological break in their family.

While Dan and Beth grow gradually dissimilar in their appearance, Alex and Beth begin echoing each other more strongly. The night of the book party Beth appears in a black suit with a low neckline, which looks like a slightly more conservative version of what Alex wears, a shimmery black dress with a plunging v-neck that stops below her breasts. Their hair, while different colors, is actually styled similarly, appearing teased and high, and Beth's hair gets bigger and more out of control as the narrative proceeds, thus mimicking Alex's medusa-like locks. That the two women double in this way suggests again how color in the film is used as a configuration; while they are meant to represent opposing poles, the women shadow each other visually and psychologically throughout the narrative. Each woman owns a white terrycloth robe (Beth wears hers the night of Alex's final attack) and in that climactic death duel both women are wearing white.

These configurations establish themselves so well because *Fatal Attraction*'s colors are by and large drab or washed out; the film's monochromatic palette consists mainly of blacks, whites, warm blues and oranges. However, red participates in this schema as well, although as an outlier to this palette, it signals something dire or unexpected.[3]

Alex's long red fingernails are, for instance, a giveaway to her sultry danger, and Dan's ensnarement in this world is visually recorded when he, after leaving her apartment the morning after their first night together, is bathed in an intense red light. His imbrication in Alex's realm is gestured to as well when a shock of red blood appears on Dan's face after Alex's suicide attempt. Audiences see the blood before Dan does, as she embraces him and smears her blood on him, which he does not initially know. Shock cuts reveal her bloody wrists, and the red again stands out against her all-white shirt, apparel not dissimilar to a straitjacket. In Lady Macbethian fashion, Dan's face and hands are stained with Alex's blood, a symbol perhaps of her intention to make his sin visible and punishable.

While the blood here signals a death wish, the film at times uses red in more playful ways, namely by linking blood to the wine and spaghetti sauce the couple consumed earlier that same evening. In another gesture of deliberate doubling, Beth, like Alex, makes Dan spaghetti, and twice Beth reminds him that she has left it in the fridge. However, for Dan the price of eating Alex's spaghetti rather than his wife's is quite steep – before the night is over, Dan will not only consume Alex's spaghetti sauce, but also find himself bathed in her blood. The film's sly joke that the red spaghetti sauce can transmogrify into blood signals how quickly the domestic can turn deadly, since the appetizing turns nauseating, not unlike the affair. As soon as Alex's red blood appears it is already too late for Dan to extract himself from her clutches; indeed, the only escape lies, in the end, in *her* bloody death. Dan, of course, does take temporary measures to whitewash the evidence of his crimes against the family – the incriminating uneaten spaghetti is fed to the family dog, Alex's scent is vanquished by a shower, and her bloodied wrists are cleaned and bandaged. Yet, as we will see in the next section, Alex refuses to be dismissed quite so efficiently.

Sorry, Wrong Number

It is a slight exaggeration, but not a totally unreasonable assertion, to say that because the text on which *Fatal Attraction* is based organizes itself around a series of phone calls, the telephone is *the* central motif in the film. *Fatal Attraction* was conceived after producer Sherry Lansing saw James Deardan's *Diversion* (1979), a short film whose basic plot Dearden described as follows:

> A writer takes his wife to the station in the morning with their child and sees them off. Then he picks up the phone and rings a girl whose number he's got. He takes her out to dinner, takes her to bed. He thinks that's the end of it, but the phone rings the next day and it's her. So he goes over to see her and spends Sunday with her. And Sunday evening she freaks out completely and cuts her wrists ... He stays the second night and gets home early in the morning. His wife gets back. The phone rings and it's the girl. He fobs her off and the phone rings again and the wife goes to pick up the phone and you know that's going to be it. She's going to find out about the affair. The wife picks up the phone and says hello, and the screen goes black. (Quoted in Faludi, 1991: 117)

Diversion's director Dearden was later employed to write the screenplay for *Fatal Attraction*, and this description of his earlier film highlights the ubiquity of the phone in both *Diversion*'s and *Fatal Attraction*'s renderings of scorned women who use this technology to wreak havoc on their wayward lovers and their families.[4] Phone terror has, of course, myriad variations, and classical American cinema has famously featured phones that will not stop ringing, callers who seem to know too much about what the receiver is doing and saying, and even characters who accidentally overhear plans for their own murder. In *Fatal Attraction* the phone's presence turns too on the question of communication, as if to advertise its twofold, self-contradictory promise – while inviting proximity, the phone simultaneously and often perversely denies precisely the connection it promises to deliver.

The first phone call in *Fatal Attraction* occurs just minutes into the film's opening; tellingly, Dan does not hear it. As he listens to headphones while working on the couch, the phone rings unacknowledged until his daughter breaks in, "Daddy, telephone." This innocuous call, a simple request from a female friend to know what Beth plans to wear to the upcoming book party, coheres with the Edenic scene that opens the film. As discussed in the previous section, Dan is still innocent, and thus has no reason to fear the party on the other end of the line. Later phone calls will prove far more unsettling.

Alex's association with the phone tellingly begins from the first time she is introduced. In their initial meeting, Dan asks Alex to explain her "connection" to the book party they attend; the following Saturday morning Dan and Alex re-meet, and she mentions having called the author she represents. Later that night, she remarks to Dan that she phoned her original date to cancel, a comment that may very well be disingenuous. This association between Alex and the phone thus begins harmlessly enough, and only gradually turns ominous. Returning home on the Sunday morning after his night with Alex, Dan calls his wife's parents from his kitchen, and suddenly the phone rings again – Dan clearly expects it to be Beth. Pausing on photos of Dan, his dog, and his child, the camera lingers on the phone, signaling to the viewer what will be the first of Alex's many unwanted calls.[5] Answering unawares, Dan gets the first taste of Alex's wrath: she comments, "I woke up, and you weren't here. I hate that." Dan accuses her of not giving up, yet he palliates her when he agrees to spend the day together in the park. Dan's capitulation to this demand is however one of his many mistakes, for it gives Alex perhaps an overinflated sense of the sway that her phone calls hold. As is soon made clear, her calls will quickly lose their effectiveness.[6]

From this point on, the phone bespeaks Alex's unrelenting will and serves as a metonym for her persistency. Subsequent to their weekend together Dan makes clear his intention to extricate himself from their romance and to return to his family life, yet Alex repeatedly attempts further communication. The violation wrought by Alex's telephonic intrusions is most delicately depicted during scenes of familial intimacy or repose, such as the scene where a phone call interrupts Dan in bed with his wife. The camera pans across the bed, from a sleeping Beth to a sleeping Dan, to the clock which reads 2:13, to a black phone, which suddenly rings. Dan answers the phone and immediately begins to disguise Alex's identity with euphemistic work talk, and the scene shows Alex on a white phone pacing her apartment in a white negligee, demanding that they meet. Alex is shot from behind pillars, which look to be lining and enclosing her, a melodramatic strategy that speaks to her sense of entrapment. (Notably, this is the last phone call of Alex's that Dan actually answers.) Another time, Alex calls during a dinner party the Gallaghers are hosting and Beth answers the phone and Alex briskly hangs up. Again, the sterility of her white apartment contrasts the homey dinner scene at the Gallaghers', as old friends laugh, joke, and imbibe together.

The place that the phone holds in Dan and Alex's respective lives vividly records the contrast between them – he lives in a family that makes and receives many calls, where she presumably makes many but receives few. Likewise, for Alex the phone serves as a last desperate connection to a relationship slipping from her grasp; for Dan, Alex's presumption of intimacy via the phone goes from the unsettling to the downright disturbing. The contrastive position of the phone in each of their emotional registers is spatially rendered in the hours following Alex's suicide attempt, when Dan stays with Alex for an additional night and quietly calls his wife from Alex's phone. The scene uncovers Alex's surreptitious, observational disappointment, beginning as the camera crawls downward, past a rainy window, revealing a white phone on a table beside the bed in which Alex pretends to sleep. While her side of the apartment is sterile, uncluttered and lit in cold blue tones, Dan stands across the room in a warm alcove, calling his wife on a different phone. Like his family home, this space is cluttered with papers, books, photos and lamps, is lit in soft orange light, and includes Dan's dog, who rests comfortably asleep on the floor beside him. The camera then pans back to Alex, quietly despairing in her colorless bed, as if to emphasize that stark contrast between these two spaces. Reposing alone in a room devoid of familial accoutrements, she hears Dan tell Beth he loves her, as Dan stands in a space that seems more reminiscent of his home than Alex's. Dan is physically though not emotionally available to Alex, a fact made clear by her relegation to a lonely bed, as her unringing phone sits in silent judgment.

The torment involved in the previous scene coalesces around Alex's awareness that Dan wants to communicate with his wife and not with her. Similarly adding to this insult is the fact that, once Dan leaves

Alex's incessant calling is visually associated with her massive appetites.

Alex's apartment, the phone stands as her only connection to him. Her manic calling thereby signifies a defiant refusal of *his* declaration of inaccessibility, and accessibility is precisely what Dan's marital status denies Alex. (As Dan says, "I like you. And if I wasn't with somebody else, then maybe I'd be with you. But I am.") Their relation escalates into a battle over what degree of accessibility Dan owes Alex, and clearly she feels entitled to more than he grants. Dan's decision to change his home phone number following Alex's insistent calls wordlessly answers and rebuffs precisely this desire, and elicits an enraged response from her. Subsequent to this rejection, the film shows Alex, home alone, sitting on her bed in a black shirt and white pants, and surrounded by cartons of Häagen Dazs ice cream, Oreos, and Doritos, pleading with the operator to give her the new number, to restore her connection. Alex screams at the operator that this is an emergency, and the scene likens Alex's gorging on food with her hyper-consumption of Dan's life, using such an image in order to decry her out-of-control appetites. The technology, however, proves unyielding in that it will not answer Alex's desire for connection, and in turn highlights that Alex has few other mechanisms by which to restore her place in Dan's life. Her relation to the technology in the wake of such refusals complies with J. P. Telotte's general assertion that "the telephone represents the barriers to desire ... signaling a human *inability* to satisfy desire and overcome limitation in normal ways" (1989: 50). As Alex discovers, reaching out via the phone only to have those actions rebuffed indirectly confirms the distance between her and the family at the other end of the line.

Taken from Alex's perspective, one might argue that her attempts at communication protest the fact that the affair proceeded throughout according to the logic of Dan's schedule. When his wife was away Alex's telephonic persuasions proved effective; only when Beth returns does the phone call no longer hold sway. Taken aback by what she perceives as this sudden rejection, Alex also understands the phone call as a duty she is owed. Picking up the phone, as Avital Ronnel reminds us, places the recipient in the position of being the call's "beneficiary, rising to meet its demand, to pay a debt ... It is a question of answerability. Who answer the calls of the telephone, the call of duty, and accounts for the taxes it appears to impose" (1989: 2). Notably, Alex introduces questions of interpersonal responsibility in precisely the same terms, clearly feeling that Dan should take her calls, and that she is justified in asking him to do so. As she says, she is going to be the mother of his child, and she deserves some respect. When Dan names these behaviors sad and pathetic, she looks indignant and asks, "Well, what am I supposed to do? You won't answer my calls. You change your number. I'm not going to be *ignored*, Dan!" Here, Alex makes discursive alignment between the act of answering the telephone and the act of paying his debts, arguing that she is owed this response.

Dan's sense of the time and effort he owes Alex does not, however, extend much past their shared weekend together and thus to his mind, he has done all the "right" things. He stays the night following her suicide attempt, and when she comes to his office later that week, he sees her and wishes her well. Days later, he takes her call again at the office, when it is clear she has been calling all day. Afterwards, however, he instructs his assistant not to put her through any more. It would be a stretch to say the film condones Alex's desperate attempts at communication; instead, Dan elicits sympathy because Alex's behavior becomes unreasonable. What more, he (and we) ask, could she want from him? What more is he obliged to do? In the film's logic, Alex is the one who fails to live up to the implied contract of the one-night stand because she demands the relationship's longevity, and uses the phone to insist on its continuation. To compensate for these denials, Alex insinuates herself in increasingly more egregious and insistent ways into Dan's life, such as posing as a prospective buyer for his family's Manhattan condo, and in the process securing for herself the family's now unlisted number.[7]

Alex's determination to regain access to Dan via the phone makes use of the phone's most searing communicative potential, namely, its ability to facilitate an instantaneous, irreversible connection. This observation is reiterated by Alex's verbal reminder to Dan that the phone can upend one's life instantaneously. In a moment of rage Alex tells Dan, "I'll tell your wife," and when he threatens to kill her if she does, she screams, "It only takes a phone call!" The phone in this case becomes the technological equivalent of an outing since it does *only* take a phone call for Alex to instantly expose Dan, and in turn unravel his entire domestic life. She even begins making the call, appearing in a low-angle canted frame that bespeaks her frantic state of mind, but desists once Beth picks up, and Alex then throws the phone across the room. To have completed this call, however, would strip Alex of the one advantage she has in her and Dan's cat-and-mouse game, for she relies on Dan's dread of exposure to get him to appear at her bidding. (Dan acknowledges as much at the end of the film, when he tells Alex, via the phone, that it is over because Beth knows everything.)

The phone thus appears as the metaphorical tectonic plate of the film, consistently shifting ground beneath Dan's feet. While some calls are merely tremors, others threaten to erupt and upend his entire domestic existence. The nagging fear that the phone will obliterate his family's already precarious isolation, for instance, animates Dan's reaction to a ringing phone during the move-in process to their new house in the country. Agreeing to relocate the family in part to escape Alex and the city, Dan is visibly unnerved when the sounds of the call suddenly pierce the quiet afternoon. To emphasize his abrupt attention shift, the camera slowly zooms into a close-up of the phone, which is sitting on the staircase behind black bars, a motion that visually renders Dan's anxiety and sudden inability to focus on anything else. Abruptly and unceremoniously dropping the table he is helping to move, Dan runs to the phone and, heart in his throat, picks it up. He smiles. "Martha, Martha, It's Martha," he says three times, comically telling everyone in the house. Martha, thank god.

The close-up of the ringing phone reveals Dan's fear of who waits on the other end of the line.

The interplay between the promise of proximity and the simultaneous denial of it organizes the presentation of the phone in *Fatal Attraction*, although the film understands this motif differently for the characters of Dan and Alex. For Dan each of the phone's rings threaten exposure, while the apparatus frustrates Alex, beckoning a communication ultimately (and repeatedly) denied. The phone's presence in the film thus nicely echoes its major themes, namely the interplay between secrecy and exposure, the looming destruction of trust, and the encroaching dangers of communication that is unwanted and out of place. Not coincidentally, these themes also encapsulate the adultery narrative. Adultery in some ways is about the wrong people coming too close, as Tony Tanner contends, "adulteration implies pollution, contamination, a base admixture" (1979: 12). The phone literalizes this metaphor because it allows for such entrances, for the crossing of borders and boundaries, for the mix-up of bodies and spaces. Alex uses the phone to enter these places, to make visible the intrusion Dan's adultery has sanctioned, and in essence to try and facilitate a swap between herself and Beth.[8]

At the same time Dan's adultery discombobulates his own familial space, in the sense that it results in his displacement from his family. After Dan reveals his affair, Beth makes Dan move out of their home. The phone again records the unnatural state that adultery precipitates, since Dan can no longer communicate in person with his daughter but must now satisfy himself with a brief nightly phone call. As a suddenly single parent, Dan adopts a position of exclusion akin to

Alex's since he is now also relegated to phoning his family from an impersonal space, his pathetic hotel room bespeaking his loneliness and alienation. Adultery's ability to displace bodies from their "rightful" places is here rendered with intense pathos, in the poignant physical separation of father and daughter.

The promise that the family will recuperate, however, is also contained in condensed form in the telephone narrative. The film's second-to-last phone call rights the wrongs of unwanted intrusion, when Beth puts a final stop to the swap that Alex so desires. She tells Alex that "if you ever come near my family again, I will kill you." Notably, this is the only time we see Alex receive a phone call, and, though Dan places the call, it bespeaks a break in the exclusivity of Dan's and Alex's relation, which Dan suggests when he tells Alex that "it's over" because Beth now knows everything. Beth's symbolic entry into the phone chain thus inculcates her intervention into the adultery narrative, a disruption that proves effective insofar as she later realizes her threat to kill Alex.

Break-ins and Boiled Bunnies

Because Dan's and Alex's affair takes place in public restaurants, elevators, hallways, and dance clubs, in addition to Alex's apartment, Dan's home remains pristine, safe from the desperate, groping, animalistic sexual encounters that characterize his affair. He deliberately does not bring Alex to his home, for clearly she does not belong there or in his office space, the two places she most tries to insinuate herself following the conclusion of their weekend together. The film thereby identifies Alex as an abject figure who repeatedly enters the spaces where she is not wanted, and trains audiences to regard the sight of her with shock and suspicion. This section will categorize Alex's numerous break-ins and border violations, explaining how they collectively encourage audiences to regard Alex's mobility as pathological.

Anthropologist Mary Douglas writes of how dirt is "matter out of place" or that which we find inappropriate in a given context, a relevant conception to this section because Alex occupies precisely this position – she is the mistress, not the wife, and her appearance, post-affair, in the spaces where only the wife should reside seems like an assault. As well, this conception of dirt as merely "matter out of place" resonates with Alex's assertion that she refuses to be viewed as dispensable. As she says, "I won't allow you to treat me like some slut you can just bang a couple of times and throw in the garbage." While crass, Alex's language indicates an actual truth, since garbage defines itself as that which we have once wanted and used and then decided to expel from our homes. Like garbage, Alex goes from the desirable to the abject – Alex insinuates that she knows she is now considered not only extraneous but also disgusting, a designation she actively refuses.

Alex's demand that she not be treated like garbage is linked to her repeated demand that she be accommodated in spaces where she wants to go (rather than those to which she is invited). Her insistence on precisely this sort of mobility unites the film's most metonymic moments, for in their own way each records her successful imbrication into spaces where *she* wants to be. Alex's sinister quality resides in her ability both to appear unexpectedly and to make her presence known when she has not been seen. An exemplary moment of the former occurs, for instance, through a point of view shot that greets Alex's sudden visit to Dan's law office; the viewer cannot help but share Dan's shock and surprise upon seeing her sitting in his office in a stark black coat. Because no visual or sound cues indicate Alex's presence before the sight of her is granted, viewers are as unaware and unprepared as Dan to deal with her arrival.

The camera plays a similar trick when Dan enters his apartment and finds Alex posing as a prospective buyer for the family's Manhattan condominium. As in the office scene, the film deliberately aligns the viewer with Dan's perspective – we begin following Dan crossing a dangerous and busy intersection, where he almost gets hit by a car. Audiences then encounter Alex at the same time he does, as he hears familiar voices and walks into his living room aghast to find his jilted lover amicably having tea with his unsuspecting wife. Point of view shots feature both Alex and his wife looking directly at him (usually characters are at a slight angle from the camera); thus the technique conveys an eerie sense of visual assault. Both women gaze at him the same way, making their separate identities somewhat indistinguishable. The blocking of the scene also records the exchangeability of the two women as they sit side by side on the couch, and the triangulation of the relation between Dan, Alex, and Beth is evidenced at the end of the sequence as Dan first stands between the two women, and then stands with Alex, bifurcated by Beth. Deviously, Alex also uses this opportunity to trick Beth into writing out the couple's now-unlisted phone number, a maneuver that spurs Dan to retaliate by appearing at her apartment. Yet, unlike Alex's unwanted intrusion, his visit serves as an almost perverse capitulation to Alex's desire for attention – Alex treats this visit as a social call and begins by offering Dan the drink of his choice.[9]

Certainly, the most memorable break-in of the film is the one we never see happen outright, although its bloody aftermath comprises the film's most iconic moment. *Fatal Attraction*'s intentionally jarring image of Whitey's bloody body peering out from its watery grave gave rise to the now-well recognized term "bunny boiler," and Alex's murderous act has come to be associated with the film writ large.[10] The fact that Alex chooses to boil the bunny speaks acutely to her refusal to concede to the Gallaghers the pastoral seclusion that their county home supposedly affords. Dan buys and transports the bunny to his daughter only after they have moved, and the scene where he calls Beth to tell her that the bunny is coming home shows her painting the family hallway. Alex's murder of the bunny thus dramatically assaults the sense of safety supposedly offered by this bucolic setting, and in doing so she turns the Gallaghers' fantasy of being better able to control intrusion while in the country into something of an ironic joke. To wit: the Gallaghers are just as vulnerable in the country as they were in the city, and perhaps even more so because of the lack of neighborly surveillance.

The scene where Alex's murderous break-in is revealed highlights this sense of eerie isolation, and the tension of this scenario is heightened especially by the editing sequence that introduces it. The Gallagher family is returning home from an afternoon with Beth's parents, and the scene begins with a shot of their car pulling into the driveway, as the family tumbles out, the dog barks, and birds chirp in the late-afternoon autumn air. The tone turns ominous, however, when the camera pans the interior of the empty Gallagher home, then remains stationary as Beth enters and begins turning on lights. The initial pan of the house has the intended effect of suggesting a presence in the house other than the entering Beth, and as discussed, the film repeatedly enunciates the myriad ways in which the sanctity of the Gallagher home has been violated. The bunny scene elliptically echoes these other scenes of domestic intrusion, although here the violation is perhaps even more personal: not only has Alex foraged through the Gallaghers' yard to collect Whitey, she has entered and cooked in the Gallaghers' *kitchen*, the primary site of female domesticity. Yet, the scene focuses not so much on the action of the break-in as on its terrifying aftermath, since Beth's attention is drawn to the kitchen where a stew pot sits atop a gas stove, boiling water streaming out from underneath the lid. Boiling water is also a structuring motif in the film, and its use here echoes other scenes that feature boiling teapots and coffeepots. Beth's eyeing of the pot and the eyeline match that shows the pot begin with mild curiosity, but the editing pace increases the tension and suspense, since precisely as Beth registers the pot and begins to walk toward it the film cuts to a tracking shot of Ellen running through their yard, en route to visit Whitey. Ellen's footsteps, crunching on the grass, echo through the shot, which then cuts to a zoom-in on the boiling pot and then a zoom-in on the rabbit hutch, motions which visually communicate each of the Gallagher females' more concentrated attention on the objects before them. As Beth walks closer to the stove the shots alternate between images of her and images of what she sees, as her awareness that something is amiss grows steadily stronger. The climax of this sequence occurs when Beth begins lifting the top of the pot, and the shot cuts to Ellen yelling, "Daddy!" Dan appears on screen in a reaction shot saying, "What?" and Beth opens the pot and screams. Mimicking the horror of these discoveries and further marking Dan as a powerless bystander to them, the camera zooms in on the bunny's bloody body, zooms in on Dan, who hears the screams, goes back to a shot of Beth screaming, then to a shot of Ellen yelling, "Whitey's gone!", then back to Beth yelling, "Dan!", and then finally to Ellen yelling, "Whitey's gone!" The crosscutting technique here adopts a dual point of view insofar as it

The film skillfully crosscuts between Beth and Ellen's gruesome discoveries.

reflects both Beth's and Ellen's state of mind, and confirms that the two discoveries happen at the same moment and lead to equally terrified reactions. As if to underscore the trauma, the next shot is of Ellen in bed, virtually comatose with grief.

The scene shrewdly uses the crosscutting technique to effect immediacy and urgency; as well, its pathos derives from its reminder that Alex's single act of treachery creates multiple and simultaneous victims. As Mary Ann Doane reminds us, quoting and translating Jacques Goimard, "the pathetic is produced more easily through the misfortunes of women, children, animals, or fools" (1991: 286). The bunny scene in *Fatal Attraction* notably involves all these, relaying as it does the suffering of Beth (the woman), Ellen (the child), Whitey (the animal), and Dan (arguably, the fool). Tellingly, however, the man is spared the immediate horror; though implicated in both scenarios, Dan is left powerless in each. Beth yells for Dan, and Ellen screams, "Daddy!", verbal invocations that make clear the responsibility he bears for having created this domestic nightmare. Yet at the same time Dan remains unable to stop the invasion, the cruelty that ensues, or the deadly discoveries to which both females are simultaneously subject. Chapter Four considers the film's reactionary view of adultery as a scourge that threatens the security of the middle-class family, but here it is useful to think about how the spatial logic of the bunny's discovery highlights Dan's impotence in the face of his family's obvious suffering. As he stands immobile in the middle of his yard, the blocking of the bunny scene underscores Dan's paralysis. Present beside neither his wife nor his daughter, Dan does not protect either family member from their twin traumas. In this way, the film provides visual recognition of the ineffectualness that plagues Dan for the duration of the film.

In much the same way, Beth and Ellen (rather than Dan himself) bear the burden of unwanted intrusions in the scene where Alex takes Ellen to the deserted fairground, and again, the Gallagher females suffer far more viscerally than does Dan. Beth, not Dan, goes to pick up Ellen from school, only to find her missing, and Ellen endures this afternoon, complete with a terrifying ride on a roller coaster that hardly seems age appropriate. Tellingly, the scene deliberately doubles Beth and Alex, the real mother versus the fake mother, and in turn identifies Alex as an interloper who endangers rather than protects the child. Constructed in such a way as to invite sympathy for Beth and Ellen, the scene identifies them as the innocent victims who must live a nightmare on Dan's behalf. Shot from Beth's point of view, Beth's entry into the school is greeted with quizzical looks from Ellen's teachers, who say that Ellen has already been picked up. Hearing this, Beth immediately begins running down the hallway. Instantly frenetic, the pace matches Beth's increasing tension since the camera speeds up, tracking in back of her, both on her way into the classroom (where Ellen's classmate says simply, "She's gone") and again as she leaves. The scene continues from the perspective of inside Beth's car, and the shots alternate between close-ups of Beth's worried face and frantic point of view shots that register what she sees as she turns her head from left to right, scouring the streets for signs of her missing daughter.

As if to answer her desperation, the sequence cuts to a long shot of Playland, and Alex appears in profile, walking hand in hand with Ellen, as carnival music plays in the background. In a quick crosscut, Beth bursts through the front door of the Gallagher home, now screaming, "Ellen!" and the camera tracks inside an ice cream parlor, where Alex buys Ellen an ice cream. The scene again cuts back to Beth, who bounds up the stairs in her home, appearing in a canted frame that visually marks her sense of panic. The crosscutting mimics the frantic intensity of the bunny scene, and it continues as Beth runs back down the stairs, which the camera records in a high angle shot that both emphasizes Beth's powerlessness and renders her home instantaneously eerie. Devoid of Ellen, the home becomes the setting of a domestic nightmare, as it will also be at the film's climax. Cutting to an establishing shot of the roller coaster, then one of Alex and Ellen on the ride, the film correlates Beth's frantic search with the fearful anticipation of roller coaster thrills. Yet, in contrast to Beth, Alex and Ellen remain stoic; wind blowing in her hair, Alex looks at Ellen, who sits impassively on the ride. The sequence includes point of view shots which reflect Alex and Ellen's view of the roller coaster car ratcheting up the hill, and shots of Beth frantically driving her car. The editing sequence thereby visually links the frenetic winding up of the roller coaster to Beth's increasing desperation, as she drives in an increasingly reckless fashion.

Deliberately, spectators are taken along for both the car and roller coaster "rides," yet, because the unstoppable motion of the car mimics that of the roller coaster, the pace and energy are not so much exhilarating as they are terrifying. Alex and Ellen eventually begin screaming, their pleasurable fear a shallow mockery of Beth's heart-wrenching despair as she asks, over and over, "Ellen, where are you?" Towards the end of the sequence, the graphic matching is also unmistakable: Alex braces for the roller coaster's terrifying descent, her neck muscles clenched, and a moment later, Beth braces for a car crash, since she cannot stop in time to avoid rear-ending a station wagon at a stoplight. The next time we see Beth, she is battered and bruised, lying in a hospital bed, much as Ellen reclined in bed following Whitey's untimely demise.

Collectively, these scenes of unwanted intrusion use editing to increase tension and suspense; as well, they portray Alex as an unstoppable source of kinetic destruction. The final section examines this kinesis by evaluating the importance of water to the film, and focuses in particular on how water encapsulates Alex's sexiness as well as her danger.

Bathrooms, Water, Sex, and *Psycho*

Fatal Attraction is a film literally oozing with fluids – rain, blood, tap water, acid, and vomit all make visible appearances. As discussed in the next chapter, the film further associates these fluids with Alex, as they help to identify her as a monstrous presence. However, the most salient of these fluids in *Fatal Attraction* is water, a substance not so much abject as it is sexually suggestive. A downpour spurs Dan and Alex to an impromptu dinner following a business meeting, for instance, and water noticeably accompanies *Fatal Attraction*'s first sex scene. Pushed up against the sink of her Manhattan loft, Alex reaches behind her to turn on the faucet, and repeatedly splashes water on her face, Dan's, and on her breast. The water continues to run as they have sex, and the couple fumble their way to the bedroom, Dan's pants down around his ankles. The scene highlights Dan's status as a bumbling lover and yet also serves as an erotic release, a sensation indicated by the fact that the shot cuts to a camera pan of the stove, where an old-fashioned coffee pot percolates. Unmistakably correlating the tap water and this now boiling water with sex, the film uses water as a shorthand for desire.

Heating water involves provoking it to the point that it is turbulent and irate, an observation the film mines shortly thereafter when Alex cuts her wrists following Dan's attempt to leave her on Sunday night. When Dan realizes what she has done, the moment is accompanied by loud, pounding kettle drums which underscore the rapid shift in the scene's emotional tenor. Taking her over to the sink, Dan forces Alex's hand under water as she screams in pain. While the running water previously bespoke an instance of sexual intrigue, it, like the spaghetti sauce, quickly turns sinister; suddenly bearing the charge of washing away blood, the water needs to salve the passion and the fury that the sex ignited. Subsequently, Dan runs around the house, a canted frame signaling his sense of panic and surprise, and he administers to her wounds in Alex's bathroom as rain pours and thunder rolls outside the window. The film thus makes the association between Alex, water, and passion explicit; as Kerstin Westerlund-Shands argues, Alex represents "Dionysian, or chthonian forces, forces connected with the caprices of nature, with uncontrollable eruptions, with overflowing liquidity, with sexuality, fertility, and reproduction, as well as with death" (1993: 115).

By pairing sex and suicide the film invokes a psychoanalytic chain of associations that link the sex drive to the death drive. Following Alex's kidnapping of Ellen, for instance, Dan forces his way into the apartment and brutalizes Alex, chasing her around and almost strangling her. The wild abandon of the earlier sexual encounter and especially its lawless quality transmogrifies into a desperate attempted murder – in both scenarios Alex makes Dan lose control, and the couple mutually sweat and gasp for breath. In the frantic chase around the apartment, they destroy furniture, overturn a bike, and break glass, and the scene's first climax occurs when Dan begins strangling Alex, his hands around her neck. He eventually lets go, and their panting exhaustion following this chase mimics the deep breaths that followed their love making. After the chase, Alex splashes water on her face from her sink, just as she did in the earlier sex scene, then grabs a knife from the kitchen, attempting to stab Dan. Water saturates this scene, and eventually Dan wrenches the knife away from her and leaves it on the counter. As in their first sex scene, no words are exchanged between the couple. Their bodies speak passion, lust, and later hatred, yet the twinning of these scenarios confirms the inextricability and perhaps even the indistinguishability of desire and destruction. Commenting on the attack scene's final shot of Alex smiling wanly as she pins her body up against a wall, Emily Fox Kales writes that "Alex's face takes on a smile of gratification as if she has just had an orgasm" (2003: 1633). Whether ravaging each other in passion or in hatred, the characters engage in a similar emotional and physical dynamic.

Water also makes a number of subtle appearances throughout the film's diegesis – Alex cooks Dan's spaghetti in a pot of water (a pot not unlike the one in which the rabbit dies), Dan showers to clean off the traces of Alex from his body, and Alex and Beth share tea when she visits the family's condo. The perseverance of the water motif comes to a head, however, in the film's final sequence, a series that quotes what have already become the film's signature moments and iconic images. The scene begins with a pan across the Gallaghers' foggy yard at dusk and stops at the house, where this time an orange light goes on in an upstairs bedroom. Notably, no one is there to pull a shade down. Dan, dressed in a white shirt and black pants, tucks his daughter into bed, and she too is dressed all in white, with an off-white-colored stuffed pony beside her. Shortly thereafter we see close-up shots of the water Dan runs from the faucet for Beth's tea. As he waits for the water to boil, Dan's oblivion echoes those of earlier scenes where he is not where he should be, as he casually eats one of his daughter's fruit rollups in the living room at the same time that his wife fights for her life upstairs. Because Beth is being terrorized in the bathroom, she does not turn off the faucet and the bathtub overflows, to the point that water, like rain, drips down through the ceiling to the first floor. Again, Dan notices it but does nothing. Only when Dan removes the blaring teapot, whose loud whistles have been drowning out Beth's screams, does he realize what is happening on the floors above him.

The most water-logged image of the film is, of course, Beth's final scene in the all-white bathroom, where she prepares to take a bath. As in *Psycho*, there are multiple close-up shots of running water. As well, the sight of a near-naked woman left alone in the bathroom underscores

The close-ups of faucets and drains in *Fatal Attraction* recall Hitchcock's *Psycho*.

her vulnerability, as does the fact that Beth sports a cast on her already broken wrist. In this steam-filled room, Beth studies her reflection, examining her black eye in the round shaving mirror, and then flips the mirror around to get an even more magnified view, right before Dan enters the bathroom to see if she needs anything. (Here, the close-up of Beth's eye seems to deliberately echo the final shot of Marion's lifeless eye in *Psycho*'s shower sequence.) After Dan has returned downstairs, Beth handles a glass jar, and wipes away steam from the larger bathroom mirror. Suddenly, Alex's face behind her becomes visible, which causes Beth to drop and break the glass. Both women are dressed in white, and this image of Alex as a quiet doppelgänger to Beth is registered in an almost Bergman-like shot of their two faces in the mirror, an image that speaks to Alex's repeated attempts to take Beth's place. Naomi Segal comments on the overlap between the two women here, writing that: "Of course this types the outsider as both intervening on and belonging inside the scheme she ruptures. Beth is potentially the same sort of woman as Alex ..." (1997: 202).

Following the shot of the two women in the mirror together, a cut reveals Alex standing in the doorway to the bathroom holding a knife, the same knife, in fact, that she attacked Dan with in her apartment. She grazes her leg with it, and her blood begins dripping on her feet and the bathroom floor. The knife attack, as Alex and Beth scuffle on the bathroom floor, also echoes Alex's previous attack on Dan in her apartment. The knife eventually goes sliding out of reach across the bathroom floor, as the two women kick and claw each other. Downstairs, Dan finally lifts the teapot, hears the screams, and summarily drops the teapot, although it appears that the teapot has also burned his hand, such that its heat causes this reaction as much as Beth's distress. Dan then enters the bathroom, slams the back of Alex's head on the mirror that doubled the women, and holds her down underwater in the tub, just as he tried to strangle her earlier in her apartment. In this shot, Alex's eyes pop out, and blood bubbles out from her open mouth. Taken together, the motions of struggle, suffocation, and strangulation suggest that though they are locked in a death battle, the characters' behaviors are also highly reminiscent of the physicalities of sex – these are all, in fact, bodies pushed to the limit.

The effect of this final scene, in fact, is to turn the entire Gallagher home into a watery prison/grave. At one point before the attack Dan enters the bathroom to talk to Beth, but he is shot from a low angle behind the bars of a staircase, an image that clearly invokes that of a prison. Likewise, though Dan deliberately locks the doors to the house, audiences learn later that Alex is already in the house, thus he effectively locks her in, not out. This transmogrification of the ordinary into the deadly haunts the entire sequence, since the innocent drawing of a bath turns into the site of a bloody attack. Even when the ordeal appears to be over, subsequent to Dan's strangulation of her, Alex rises back out of the tub, a specter of the "not dead."[11] In *Fatal Attraction*, the bathtub was in actuality a four-foot-deep tub specially built for the set, a fact which explains how Alex's reemergence feels like she has lifted herself out of a coffin. When Alex comes back to life with a great gasp of breath and goes after Dan, Beth, from nowhere, comes into the bathroom, shoots Alex in the chest with a gun, and then Alex slides down the bathroom wall, leaving a bloody trail on the white walls behind her.[12] Though Dan earlier opened the drawer and revealed that the family owned a gun, the fact that Beth is the one to use it symbolically gives Beth the phallus. Though Alex's intensity has been juxtaposed throughout the film with Beth's serenity and composure, in this final scene Beth reveals herself as capable of the same murderous impulses. Her earlier verbal challenge to Alex that she will "kill her" if Alex comes near Beth's family again appeared initially idiosyncratic and unexpected, given the nature of Beth's character. Yet, as this final sequence confirms, Beth's gruesome promise was not an idle threat. The scene instead identifies Beth as capable of the same atrocities as her nemesis since Beth kills (at least in part) to hang on to an unfaithful husband, which raises the question whether her desperation for domestic security is any different from Alex's.

Alex dies like the bunny, in a bloody, watery grave, and her positioning quotes the dead bunny, as her body submerges and her head tilts over the side of the tub, just as Whitey's did over the side of the boiling pot. Thematically, the fact that Beth is the one who kills Alex, even though Dan mistakenly thinks he has, emphasizes his repeated impotence in the face of Alex's reign of terror. It also underscores the film's centralization of a battle of femininities – despite his efforts, Dan is incapable of blocking Alex's many intrusions. In turn, Dan's paralysis offers a somewhat counterintuitive comment on adultery as a masculinizing act; although it might initially seem like a testament to his virility, its aftermath repeatedly leaves his family open to penetration, and relegates Dan to multiple positions of passivity. The various images and motifs catalogued in this chapter all synergize in service of turning the ordinary into a domestic nightmare, since the film is punctuated by moments where mundane spaces and locales suddenly turn deadly. While we have atomized these various themes and devices for invoking intrusion from a technical perspective, the next chapter examines how these motifs quote and borrow from various American genre formulas. In doing so, it connects the film's domestic explorations, its intense suspense, and its emphasis on graphic sexuality to wider trends in American cinema.

Chapter 2

American Genres in *Fatal Attraction*

Fatal Attraction's graphic depictions of base instincts, rogue desires, and murderous consequences – and the number of copycat films that followed in its wake – prompted critics to credit *Fatal Attraction* with having inaugurated a new film genre aptly described as the "erotic thriller." In a comment consistent with the logic of sexuality which organizes the erotic thriller, Douglas Keesey characterized it as a form whereby "desire and death interpenetrate" (2001: 44). Likewise citing *Fatal Attraction*'s role in concretizing the genre, Linda Ruth Williams observes: "Following the success of *Fatal Attraction*, the word 'fatal' became synonymous with the genre and a metonym not for 'fate' (the inevitability of destiny) but deadly sex" (2005: 9). Yet, despite the multiple assertions that *Fatal Attraction* effectively hybridizes porn and the thriller and thus identifies itself as the ur-text for the erotic thriller, that designation only partially accounts for the film's genre affiliation, which has been alternatively labeled as a neo-noir, a melodrama, and a horror picture. Consider: the film's centralization of an ineffectual male protagonist, seduced and overpowered by a mysterious blonde woman in an urban location clearly nods to the film noir; on the other hand, the film's focus on the family as a main source of conflict and tension and its privileging of interior spaces invokes the melodrama. Because *Fatal Attraction* samples from some of the most recognizable and widely successful film genres, the film complies with and illustrates film scholar Christine Gledhill's contention that all films participate "in genres of one kind or another – and usually, several at once" (1999: 147).

Borrowing from these genres and capitalizing on their strongest and most widely recognizable features, *Fatal Attraction* exhibits a strategy of postmodern montage, one that accrues levels of generic meanings – and rewards knowing spectators – who recognize its debt to American film history.[1] Taking this cinematic history into account, this chapter organizes itself by attenuating to four major generic categories (melodrama, horror, film noir, and the erotic thriller), labels that each describe, but can not fully encapsulate, *Fatal Attraction*. For instance, props such as knives, blood, and boiling water produce suspense and even revulsion common to the horror film, yet they also underscore the film's steamy union of sex and death, a key motif in the erotic thriller. To unpack the film's hybridity, this chapter locates the distinctive features of each genre, explaining how distinctive tropes and motifs are combined anew in *Fatal Attraction*. The discussion begins with the melodrama, which is perhaps the least obvious of the genres to which *Fatal Attraction* belongs, but is nevertheless one whose principles and preoccupations significantly inform the film.

Melodrama, Music, and Windows

Cinematic melodrama relies on a strategy of heightened visual expression; extreme emotional states are refracted through props, setting, costume and location in order to speak the emotion that characters either cannot, or will not, express. Often this melodramatic sensibility results in a mise en scène that is decidedly unrealistic or over the top in some way, and melodramas are typically identified by their swelling music, lush colorations, and expressive sets. Though *Fatal Attraction* arguably has an understated rather than overinflated look, it too frequently displaces emotions onto inanimate objects (especially phones and water) which in turn stand in for extreme states of passion and desperation. As Geoffrey Nowell-Smith writes,

> What is characteristic of the melodrama, both in its original sense and in the modern one, is the way excess emotion is siphoned off. The undischarged emotion which cannot be accommodated within the action … is traditionally expressed in music and in the case of film, in certain elements

of the mise en scène. That is to say, music and mise en scène do not heighten the emotionality of an element of an action: to some extent they substitute for it. (1991: 272)

As discussed previously, the phone is the key element in *Fatal Attraction*'s mise en scène and becomes a repository for all of Dan's condensed, pressurized feelings, which range from guilt to fear of disclosure to annoyance at Alex's persistence. The insistent jarring ring vocalizes Dan's increasingly desperate entrapment, a sense he cannot share with his family. The only time Dan admits to his desperation verbally is to do so to his friends or the police, where his use of veiled terms, euphemisms, and hushed tones betray his fear of exposure. Simultaneously, the phone speaks to Alex's violent energy, her accusation that she is not being listened to, and her demand that she be heard. For her, the phone substitutes for voice, for even when Alex does not say anything during these calls their violent intrusions perpetuate and impose her will. In this way, Alex's utilization of the phone coheres with J. P. Telotte's insight that the phone both represents desire and simultaneously thwarts it; as he writes, "the telephone particularly embodies both desire and its limitations, the impulse to acquire, possess, or control other people and things, and the sense of how much we are ourselves already acquired, possessed, or controlled by the very nature of desire" (1989: 51). Indeed, the phone is perhaps the best indicator in the film of Alex's forbidden longing. As such, it speaks more acutely to this sensibility than she does herself.

Melodramas also characteristically siphon excess emotion into music, which in turns stands in for character desire. While *Fatal Attraction* features a relatively minimalist score, the film's reliance on Puccini's opera *Madame Butterfly* in two key scenes underscores its melodramatic affinities. In the sequence where Alex cooks a pasta dinner for Dan the two discover they share a passion for Puccini. Dan rhapsodizes about the experience of having gone to the opera with his father, who comforted a then five-year-old Dan frightened by the revelation that Butterfly will shortly die. As Dan admits, this was one of the few times he remembers feeling loved by his father. Alex professes a similar affinity for *Madame Butterfly*, naming it as her favorite.

Unsaid but implied is the suggestion that Dan's presence in her apartment represents an analogous state for Alex, perhaps one of the few times that *she* has felt loved. Mimicking the doomed heroine in *Madame Butterfly*, a Japanese woman who commits suicide after being seduced, impregnated, and abandoned by her American soldier lover after World War II, Alex slits her wrists the same night, in a desperate plea to convince Dan not to abandon her. The opera's poignant tragedy, conveyed through a swelling, overpowering aria, now speaks as well to Alex's trauma and provides a bridge between Alex and Butterfly, her literary doppelgänger.

Puccini's evocation of the perpetually suffering woman informs Alex's conception of her affair, a sensibility nicely conveyed through a sequence that takes place after Alex invites Dan to a production of *Madame Butterfly* at the Metropolitan Opera House. Dan politely rejects the offer, and on what audiences assume is the night of the production, the film crosscuts between Alex slumped down on the floor of her apartment, listening to Puccini, and the object of her affections blithely enjoying an evening of bowling with his wife and their best friends. The unused tickets rest beside the stereo in Alex's apartment, and the scene reverberates with the swells of *Madame Butterfly*, connecting the two sequences through a sound bridge. The operatic score thus succeeds in making Alex, planted on the floor in a white shirt mindlessly turning a light on and off, an (albeit remote) witness to Dan's exuberant bowling excursion, her loneliness and disappointment a sober contrast to Dan's thoughtless partaking in a night of family fun. Associated with Alex's desire and drives, the opera stands in for Alex's voice and effectively speaks her feelings of desperation and desertion.

Because scenes such as this afford Alex a metaphorical voice, they present a perhaps surprising opening for spectators to read Alex's subjectivity into the film. While *Fatal Attraction*'s creators repeatedly proclaimed their sense that they wanted audiences to see Alex as worthy of empathy, the film rarely bears this out, preferring instead to cultivate audience identification with Dan, who emerges as the powerless victim of her (largely inexplicable) wrath.[2] The reliance on melodramatic strategies, however, has the effect of paradoxically

Alex spends the night alone listening to *Madame Butterfly*, with her unused opera tickets by her side. Meanwhile, an oblivious Dan enjoys a night of bowling fun.

priming audiences to at least momentarily share Alex's point of view, since they identify Alex as a victim of her forbidden desires. Melodramas depict situations where desire is attached to an unattainable object, and one way to read this genre is to notice that "melodrama aligns itself with the delineation of a lack of social power and effectivity so characteristic of the cultural positioning of women" (Doane, 1991: 286). While Doane emphasizes that mothers are those who typically suffer in their desires, silent and unseen, in fact, Alex too takes on this position, particularly when she looks in the window of the Gallaghers' country house after following Dan home on the night she pours acid on his car. While audiences have presumably spent the previous ten minutes appalled by Alex's ruthless act of destruction and orally assaulted by the accusations contained in her taped rantings, the film breaks from this assignment of Alex as a heartless saboteur long enough to attest to the authenticity of her pain. The veracity of the emotion is confirmed by the fact that the sequence concludes with her watching through the window as Dan brings a long-awaited rabbit home to his eager daughter. Standing outside, Alex peers in at the three Gallaghers, who form a circular chain of affection, and the soundtrack features the hauntingly somber music that is its usual refrain. Faced with the specter of the family's happiness, Alex involuntarily vomits in the bushes. Much like the scene where Alex sits home alone with her unused opera tickets, the moment turns into an uncharacteristically sympathetic account of her thwarted hopes, the suggestion being that a now-pregnant Alex is made sick by the realization that Dan's harmonious family life has no place for her in it.

As registered on her face as she looks through the window, Alex's silent yearning connects her to a long line of cinematic women who stand desiring what lies on the other side of the glass. Paradigmatic melodramatic moments in this vein include: the stunning last scene of *Stella Dallas* (1937), where the eponymous heroine stands outside in the rain, watching her daughter get married; repeated shots of Cary Scott, the lonely widow in *All That Heaven Allows* (1955), looking at her neighborhood from inside the house that has become her cloister; the scene where *Imitation of Life's* (1935) rejected Delilah contemplates her daughter from behind the plate glass store inside which Peola now passes for white; the relegation to invisibility experienced by a young Lisa in *Letter from an Unknown Woman* (1948), when she stands behind a glass door and gazes at Stefan, the object of her life-long unrequited love; and the shot of Iowa housewife Francesca's hand gripping the door of her husband's truck as she watches through the windshield while Robert, her lover and soul mate, drives away forever in *The Bridges of Madison County* (1995). In each of these moments, the desiring heroine's gaze captures the object of her affection at the same time that it betrays the impossibility of her desire's fulfillment. While each of these women longs in some way for the life on the other side of that window, whether it be a wish for freedom or a more stable domesticity, in each case the glass serves as a barrier that both illustrates and simultaneously precludes the heroine from entering the frame she sees. Akin to the upper-class wedding wherein a spontaneous and loud woman like Stella Dallas does not fit, Dan's home life will make no accommodation for Alex, the scorned career woman whose inability to participate in the cozy familial scenario is justified by her contrastive lack of domesticity. Apparently unfit for the role of wife and mother, Alex's exclusion from the scene turns on the fact that another woman already occupies this symbolic and literal space.[3]

By inviting audience sympathy for Alex, the film could be said to balance "different points of view, so that the spectator is in the position of seeing and evaluating contrasting attitudes within a given theoretical framework – a framework which is the result of the total configuration and therefore inaccessible to the protagonists themselves" (Elsaesser, 1991: 88). The scene at the window bears out Elsaesser's idea that melodrama accommodates multiple and even divergent viewpoints in the sense that Alex is, for this brief moment anyway, uncharacteristically humanized. This is one of the few scenes when the film sustains her point of view, thereby opening up the possibility for an alternative reading of some of her other, more maniacal behaviors. Only after Dan rejects the news of her pregnancy and rejects her, in fact, do Alex's behaviors turn vengefully destructive. One might therefore read these acts of violence as responses to the disappointment instigated by having her desires so unequivocally denied. As James Conlon writes of Alex, "Her trashing the car and cooking the rabbit are attacks on a concept of family that excludes her from it; her kidnapping of Ellen and attempt to kill Beth are desperate attempts to include herself in it" (1996: 409). Melodramatic discourses of inclusion and exclusion open up a way of reading Alex's retaliations as methods of claiming what has been, and continues to be, forbidden.

Examining *Fatal Attraction* through the lens of melodrama likewise allows for a reading of Dan attentive to his blocked wishes and fantasies. While Dan's home can be characterized, as I do in Chapter One, as comfortably cluttered, an expression of the easy wealth he enjoys there, Elsaesser argues that melodramas exhibit "an acute sense of claustrophobia in décor and locale" which in turn "translates itself into a restless yet suppressed energy surfacing sporadically in the action and behavior of the protagonists" (1991: 76). While Dan's home exhibits an ease of living typically associated with upper-class Americana, this small space periodically emerges as stifling, tedious, and feminized, an observation literalized by the fact that Beth's undergarments are strewn throughout the bathroom during the opening sequence. The film also gently mocks the characters with the observation that spontaneity has little space in the context of family life; when Beth blurts out the word "shit" in frustration after Ellen steals her lipstick, Ellen greets the babysitter's arrival muttering, "Shit, shit, shit" as she approaches the door.

Disciplined behavioral practice also seems to inform Dan's and Beth's relation, to the point that Dan is infantalized by the marital dynamic itself. The first thing Beth says in the film is: "You'd better get going, kiddo, we're going to be late." (While Ellen also sits in the room watching *You Can't Do That on Television*, and the term "kiddo" might suggest that Beth directs her comments toward her daughter, Ellen is not going anywhere.) In fact, all of Beth's appearances up until she leaves for the weekend identify her as a gentle harridan who keeps Dan on a tight leash: she mouths, "Let's go" to Dan at the book party, interrupting his conversation with Alex, and likewise points at the dog and asks, "Aren't you forgetting something?" upon their return home. Dan reluctantly complies only to find that, once he finishes the task, his obvious sexual desires are circumvented by the presence of his daughter in his bed; Beth's conciliatory response to Dan is: "It's just for one night, honey." Likewise, when she and Ellen leave for the country the next morning, Beth pointedly asks Dan of the dog, "You're not going to forget to walk him, are you?" (which, in fact, he does). While simple reminders all, these comments nevertheless signal the ways in which Dan is beholden to the duties of "home-making," responsibilities that in turn disrupt his natural proclivities. (Alex makes fun of him for precisely this reason; following Beth's summons at the book party, Alex comments, "Better run along.")

As Beth's admonitions suggest, the duties associated with this claustrophobic existence exponentialize the longer they are neglected; as if to emphasize this point, Dan's return home during the weekend of his affair features accompanying shots of his lonely dog, who has clearly suffered in his absence. As well, Dan must roll around in his bed so as to simulate the appearance that the space has been lived in, and he feeds the leftover spaghetti to the dog to cover the fact that he has not eaten at home all weekend. Disciplined by his living quarters, Dan's reactions highlight the fact that his family life enforces identities — namely that of a devoted husband and father who dutifully eats the food has wife has prepared and sleeps in his own bed — that lack flexibility.

The film's cinematography visually correlates with this sense of constriction, for the camera frequently crawls through the Manhattan condo's narrow corridors, emphasizing their tight interior spaces.

Multiple times, in fact, long shots of Dan in the doorway, filmed from the far end of the corridor, literalize his journey from public to private and back. The framing of the character in the doorway constructs a tension between public and private, and melodramas tend to code doorways as liminal spaces, since they, like windows, separate the social sphere from the domestic. Crossing the threshold spatializes Dan's struggle to either abandon or maintain his domestic responsibilities, and the mere act of stepping back into the home implies a return to familial identities and the rules and responsibilities they entail. (By contrast, Beth is almost always firmly ensconced *inside* a home, and the only time audiences see her enter or leave the domestic sphere is when she bursts into their family home after Ellen has been kidnapped.) This attention to the threshold between public and private illustrates how domestic structures organize, or are supposed to organize, desire, whereas the more public nature of Dan's and Alex's affair is encapsulated in their moments in the salsa club, and especially, in the notorious elevator scene when Alex performs fellatio on Dan between floors.

Reading the film as a melodrama in which interior spaces provide a visual correlative for Dan's sense of constriction also imbues his affair with a rationale that it otherwise lacks. As audiences, we might question the veracity of Dan's statement that he is lucky to be so happily married. As Alex queries, "Then what are you doing here?" If Dan is so fulfilled in his relationship, why does he betray it? On the one hand, asking that question assumes that desire obeys a logic that it perhaps does not, since the enactment of sanctioned marital sex does not preclude the enticement and excitement of other lures. Reading Dan's domestic spheres as potentially claustrophobic does, however, allow for the possibility that the cues for Dan's motivation lie in the vicissitudes of family life. If the psychological undercurrents of domestic disharmony are denied open expression for fear of toppling the "happy family" ideal, the affair can be read as a symptomatic return of the repressed, such that it exposes the carnal desires that demand suppression under the mantle of monogamous marriage.

Yet this revolt remains short lived, since Dan's minor rebellion against those strictures only serves to remind him how valuable and

In a classic melodramatic pose, Dan looks out the window of Alex's lonely apartment.

precarious these identities are, and indeed, how desperately he wants to hold onto them. In fact, directly following Alex's suicide attempt, there is a shot of Dan looking out the window of her apartment onto the urban street below. Since he has been coerced into staying the night again, Dan's gaze clearly represents a desire to get *out* of Alex's apartment; this shot is the direct inverse of Alex's look of longing as she peers *into* his life. Likewise suggesting that the affair has constricted him more than his family life ever could, after Alex announces her pregnancy, the film features a now-familiar camera tracking shot through tight spaces. This time, however, the camera crawls through the stacks of the law library at Dan's office, where he confesses his predicament in whispers to his best friend. While the shot again bespeaks Dan's sense of entrapment, the entrapper is clearly not his family but Alex, the interloper who threatens the innocent family he took for granted. Further emphasizing all that Dan has put at risk, a subsequent scene involves him getting tearful as he watches his daughter act out a proposal scene based on Longfellow's poem "The Courtship of Miles Standish," while the family visits Beth's parents. Hugging his daughter, a choked-up Dan tells her, "I love you so much."

In addition to his obvious entrapment and regret, Dan remains multiply paralyzed throughout the narrative: Alex is the affair's instigator and aggressor, and also pursues Dan in the wake of it. Dan's relegation to the position of the passive bystander even to his own life confirms his status as the "ineffectual male" in the melodramatic register, and his incompetence is overdetermined: he stubs his toe in the first scene, gets cream cheese on his nose during a business meeting, struggles with a resistant umbrella during a downpour, fails to get the waiter's attention at the restaurant where he dines with Alex, trips while taking her into the bedroom to make love, and cannot dance but for unrhythmic bobbing. Moreover, Alex outwits him when she trumps his sham heart attack with a story about how her father died that way, which she brushes off as a falsehood even though it is later revealed to be true. While these are mainly incidental guffaws, Dan is prone to more serious lapses such as failing to protect his family from Alex's many intrusions, and in fact locks his Westchester home only *after* Alex is already inside, thereby effectively locking her in, not out. As Mercer and Shingler write, paraphrasing Nowell-Smith, "melodrama's characters are noted by their inability to take action to resolve their problems," a sentiment that aptly describes Dan (2004: 22).

Reading the film's ending through melodrama also suggests an alternate reading of what is assumed to be the film's conservative endorsement of the enduring power of family values. The film closes on a framed picture of the Gallagher family, which features a smiling Beth, Dan, and Ellen, frozen in time, an image taken to indicate a return to normalcy, a testament to the staying power of the family. Yet, by reading the preceding events back into the photo, one might argue that the picture contains within it the destruction the happy family ideal has wrought. As James Conlon writes, "the violence of the previous scene has not yet faded from our emotional sight, so we see, as in a double exposure, both the family icon and the blood spilt in sacrifice to it. This is a very scary picture" (1996: 411). Rather than existing as hermetically sealed, this picture testifies to the family as a site of repression and violence and implies that what has been wrought out momentarily will not be destroyed.

Reading the picture as such also implies that the film employs a "false happy ending," a turnaround that speaks to the film's compliance with Hollywood convention at the same time that its resolution strains credulity. As Sarah Harwood notes, the picture is an old one, clearly taken before Dan's affair. She writes, "To 'fix' this family, the narrative has to rely on invoking an earlier moment, fixing time as well as damage. To believe in the restoration of the family, we have to believe that the clock can go back, that time can be stopped, even reversed" (1997: 1). While the melodrama might provide a so-called happy ending, this ending acknowledges itself more as a wish fulfillment than a truism because it defies temporal logic. As master melodramatist Douglas Sirk said, "you don't believe the happy end, and you're not really supposed to … You sense it's hopeless, even though in a very bare and brief little scene afterwards the happy turn is being indicated. Everything seems to be OK, but you well know it isn't" (Halliday, 1972: 132). Read in these terms, the final image of the reconstituted family framed in isolation in no way ensures a happy functioning unit. To use Elsaesser's terminology, the photo serves as a "cinematic counterpoint" to the story being told, as an ironic commentary on the family's inability to rehabilitate itself after such a catastrophic violation. Far more likely than familial bliss for the Gallaghers is a sequence of events that might look like this: following Alex's death, Beth will resent and distrust Dan, Ellen will be forever psychologically scarred, Dan will lose his reputation and potentially his livelihood. The frame brackets what is a surreal and ultimately unsustainable picture, an image that is perhaps more ironic than realistic.[4]

Monsters, Medusa and the Horror Film

Designating *Fatal Attraction* as a "horror" film opens similar avenues for thinking about the repression and willful blindness necessary in order to maintain the happy family ideal, especially as it concerns the designation of Alex as the classic "monster" who threatens the family and needs to be eradicated as a result. As Judith Williamson observes, "*Fatal Attraction* is fundamentally a horror film in yuppie-melodrama land; its whole structure becomes blindingly clear once you realize that the part played by the Thing/the Blob/the Bug is played by the SWW [Single White Woman]" (1993: 66). Notably, the film turns into a horror film in its second half, when Alex transforms into a seemingly unstoppable attacker. As David Ansen wrote in a *Newsweek* review, only after the discovery of Alex's pregnancy is she apparently driven over the edge, such that "the initially sympathetic nut case turns into a full-scale movie monster out of 'Nightmare on Madison Avenue'" (1987: 76).[5] Similarly, *New Yorker* reviewer Pauline Kael notes that once Alex starts behaving as if she had a right to share in the lawyer's life, "she becomes the dreaded lunatic of horror movies" (1987: 106).

As the film's monster, Alex obeys the principles of abjection, a physical and psychological construct that Barbara Creed designates as central to the horror genre. Horrors generally focus on monsters that derive their monstrous identities by unwittingly crossing borders that should be kept separate, for example, the border between the human and non-human, or the living and the dead. According to Creed, the horror genre abounds in images of abjection, substances that cross boundaries and invite horror and disgust as a result of this crossing. These include: the corpse, blood, vomit, sweat, saliva, mucous, bodily waste, tears, and putrefying flesh. At the same time, these unnatural or unwanted border crossings define what is considered monstrous; as Creed explains of all horror films, regardless of what boundaries are crossed, "the function of the monstrous remains the same: to bring about an encounter between the symbolic order and that which threatens its stability" (1993: 40). The point of the horror film is to expel the abject, or to reassert stability by ejecting the monstrous, although the abject is never fully defeated and thus never satisfactorily expelled. (As horror theorists explain, this return accounts for the fact that horror monsters rarely stay dead.) Similar conceptions inform *Fatal Attraction*, and particularly enforce an alliance between Alex and the crossing of unwanted boundaries, since she introduces a contamination that may never be fully eradicated. As explored in the previous chapter, Alex's whole being is in some ways abject because she invades the Gallaghers' home, Dan's workplace, and his intimate life, sometimes in person and sometimes via the phone. Thus, if the goal of horror is to eject the abject, to reconstitute purity and cleanliness by throwing out that which forces too close a confrontation with the body, Alex is unquestionably an abject figure. While abject substances do not flow as unchecked in *Fatal Attraction* as they do in gorier versions of the horror film, Alex nevertheless does spill blood and vomit all over the Gallaghers' literal and symbolic life. Specifically, her long red nails invoke the color of dull blood, she smears blood on Dan's face during the suicide attempt, vomits in their yard, drips blood onto their pristine bathroom floor, and streaks her innards across their white bath tile. Concerning itself with the ritual expunging of that which is abject and unclean, the film asks audiences to participate in regarding Alex, with her uninvited blood and vomit, as precisely such an unwanted guest.[6]

Alex's wild, curly hair also cues her monstrosity, a look that has led to her comparison to Medusa, whose head was famously composed of writhing snakes and whose gaze turned men to stone. The proximity of the head to the poisonous serpents suggests a woman who has no fear and whose beauty attracts men at their own peril. The film self-consciously mines the deadly effect of Medusa's gaze during Alex's first appearance in the film, when Dan's friend Jimmy (Stuart Pankin) sees her across the restaurant and she turns on him a steely and angry stare. Jimmy then comments to Dan, "If looks could kill." As Sarah Harwood reminds us, Alex does almost all of the looking in this scene: although we first see Alex from Dan's point of view, she holds and returns his gaze (1997: 121). Similarly, when Dan sits down next to Alex, she first looks at him; and, after Beth calls him away, the camera follows Alex's gaze as she watches Dan leave the party. Yet, unlike Jimmy, Dan is not immediately turned to stone when faced with Alex's look, in part because she looks at him with desire rather than vengeance. As Douglas Keesey jokes, Dan "finds her desirable because she is actively desiring; apparently, her Medusa locks harden him into something other than stone" (2001: 53). Yet, although Dan survives the literal encounter with her, the Medusa's lure still exerts itself, in the sense that Dan's life unravels completely in the wake of their affair. This dynamic ultimately fixes Dan as the one turned to stone, paralyzed by Alex's reign of terror.[7]

Psychoanalytic explanations of the power of the Medusa likewise align the sight of her with the sight of the female genitals, and Creed points out how this experience invokes castration anxiety. As Creed explains, Freud's discussion of Medusa illustrates that the concept of the monstrous-feminine, "as constructed within and by a patriarchal and phallocentric ideology, is related intimately to the problem of sexual difference and castration" (1996: 36). The film's association between Alex and knives perhaps signals the castration anxiety that Creed discusses, since Alex attacks Dan with a knife in her apartment, the same knife she later brings to the Gallagher home. Alex's castrating impulses also share a discursive investment in Dan's feminization; on her vituperative tape she rants against his masculinity, calling him a "fag" and accusing him of not even liking women. In this way, Alex both *questions and threatens* Dan's masculinity, as if to indicate that he is paradoxically already castrated, and yet at her mercy to preserve whatever manhood he still retains.

Fear of sexual difference expresses itself as well in the repulsion with which Dan regards Alex's reproductive capacities, a potentiality signaled by her sudden pregnancy. Creed notes that horror films often reveal men's unconscious fears of women's reproductive roles, a sensibility that the film supports by casting Alex's potential motherhood as monstrous, both because it is sprung on Dan (and audiences) so suddenly, and because Alex refuses Dan's entreaty to have an abortion.[8] While horror films famously punish illicit sexuality – teenagers caught in the act of having illicit sex tend to be killed in that moment, for instance – Dan paradoxically survives the sexual encounter, yet his punishment is merely delayed. In a decade whose sexual mores were shaped by AIDS panic, Dan's punishment for engaging in unsafe sex is similarly inevitable and manifests itself in the fact that Alex is allowed to become a monstrous mother, or threaten to be so, and her monstrosity stems in part from the desperation with which she approaches this possibility. Alex tells Dan that at age 36 it may be her last chance to have a baby; linking Alex's madness to her maternal compulsions, Creed writes that "the female psychotic of the extremely successful *Fatal Attraction* is ultimately shown as mad because of her voracious need to possess a child and husband" (1993: 139).

While these theories of monstrosity comply with what is now perhaps a standard feminist reading of *Fatal Attraction* because they point out the cultural prejudices which naturalize the idea that the single, thirty-something woman would be desperate and abject, other theories of horror conversely allow her to be read as a force of psychic liberation.

Robin Wood's influential theory of horror, for example, turns on the observation that modern societies are characterized by "surplus repression"; as he explains, if basic repression ensures our humanity by forcing people to exert self-control, exhibit thought, and communicate with others, surplus repression "makes us into monogamous heterosexual bourgeois patriarchal capitalists" (1986: 71). In turn, excess sexual energy that cannot be channeled into monogamy is disavowed and projected onto the Other, whereby "it can be discredited, disowned, and if possible annihilated" (1986: 73). In such a reading, sexual energy and creativity fail to be fully repressed or eradicated; instead they return in the form of the monster, or the Other, who threatens "normality." Such theorization innovatively paves the way for a more sympathetic reading of the monster, and in turn a more monstrous reading of the normal, since it transmogrifies the normal into those who project unwanted desires and drives onto the Other, who is in this case Alex. Read in accordance with this theory of horror, Alex emerges as the casualty of surplus repression, the force that ensures Dan's place as a monogamous, heterosexual, bourgeois patriarchal capitalist. As such, Alex exists as the product or fantasy of his id, thereby answering his desire for a symbolic escape from a sexually repressive social order.[9]

The fact that excess desire must be disavowed justifies the film's designation of Alex (and especially her sexuality) as, to use Wood's terms, "perverted, monstrous, and excessive" (1986: 91). Such sexuality chafes against the gentle marital sexuality that Dan and Beth appear to enjoy, yet the perversion and the excess of Dan and Alex's sexual encounter, according to Wood's paradigm, exist as a logical outcome of surplus repression. Clamping down on Dan's sexual freedom represents a necessary condition for monogamous marriage, yet the seemingly inexplicable affair confirms the presence of desires that escape containment within the marital bed and testifies to the fact that monogamy is predicated on repression. At the same time those who excite the passions, like Alex, risk relegation to the position of the monstrous Other since they unleash all that culture tries hard to repress. Eradicating Alex solves the problem of Dan's nonmarital impulses, even though she is perhaps the catalyst for (but hardly the only source of) his renegade desires.

If Alex is a casualty of surplus repression, her monstrosity exists more as an indictment of Dan and his bourgeois life than of her uncontrollable passions. More broadly, the film might be said to high-light the perverse nature of a culture which so closely intertwines social advancement, citizenship, and a healthy functioning state with the personal commitments of marriage and monogamy. In this para-digm, Dan's bourgeois society emerges as more perverse than Alex's libidinal explosions, since her predilections answer his desire for an unfiltered, hedonistic release. Apprehending Alex as just such a force of liberation, critic James Conlon argues we should praise rather than revile Alex because she embodies the passion desperately missing from Dan's life. As he describes, while Dan's home life is nourishing, it is also dull; in contrast, "With Alex there is no casual undressing, no neat folding of clothes, no practical prioritizing about what should be done before what. There is just the total urgency of passion, of flesh desperate for the closest avenue to flesh" (1996: 405). In turn, Conlan frames Dan's rejection of Alex in Woodsian terms, arguing that, "it is not Alex whom he hates and wants so violently dead; it is his own pas-sion" (1996: 410). Conlon's reading of Alex as the return of Dan's repressed passion recuperates Alex since he labels her an energizing force. However, because stooge Dan is too weak to see her as such, he eliminates a vision of what he most wants and therefore most fears.

In such recalibrations, Alex emerges as the scapegoat for Dan's anti-social desires, and her extermination accomplishes the repression and eradication of *his* innermost wants. A similarly recuperative reading of Alex's monstrosity is made possible by considering her, as does Deborah Jermyn, as a projection not of Dan's id, but rather of Beth's. Like Creed, Jermyn also relies on a discourse of abjection, but casts this border crossing as liberating rather than terrifying. Because the monstrous woman "crosses the borders other women are forced to maintain" she lives out their fantasies about escaping their place in the symbolic (1996: 255). Indeed, unlike Beth, who is confined to domestic spaces, Alex traverses public and private, urban and country locales. As a result, Jermyn believes that: "If one looks at the female psychopath as the abject of the victim/wife, then this particular mon-strous woman can be seen as the embodiment of a female dilemma, an exploration and momentary enjoyment of conflicting roles and behavior" (1996: 255). In Jermyn's formulation, Alex distinguishes herself as a woman without sexual inhibition who comes and goes as she pleases. Although many critics have highlighted the ways that Alex lacks self-possession, Jermyn argues that Beth's character is hardly more realized, for her life is "in many ways as empty as Alex's" (1996: 256). Reading Alex as the abject of the victim/wife therefore allows for a vision of Alex attuned to her mobility, and to a revision of the common attribution of Beth's life as idyllic. As this reading suggests, Alex's sexual release is enviable rather than a perversion, but because neither Dan nor Beth (the bourgeois subjects) are able to read it as such, they systematically annihilate her.

The Neo-Noir and the Femme Fatale

While Alex has repeatedly been called a monster, she also invites identification as a classic femme fatale, an iconic character type in film noir. In a typical noir, the temptation of the dark side exerts strong influence on the male protagonist, a lure embodied by the sultry and sexy femme fatale who seduces him into committing a crime on her behalf. *Fatal Attraction* salutes the noir, and almost perfectly imitates its narrative arc: Dan, the ineffectual, weak male, capitulates to the temptations of the femme fatale Alex. Criminalized by this association, only after he has succumbed to her does he become fully aware of her selfish motives and diabolical nature. Though he becomes subsequently cognizant that he prefers the stability offered by the "good girl," his wife, the aftermath of his crime haunts him and threatens to ruin his life. Thanks to this confluence of these circumstances and the genre requirements of noir, James Naremore calls *Fatal Attraction* one of the two most commercially successful noirs ever made, the other being *Basic Instinct*, which also stars Michael Douglas (1998: 264).

That the film adheres to a noir formula is a principle echoed in James Damico's writing on noir, which predates *Fatal Attraction* by a decade; Damico argued that the "narrative model" for noir dictates that a man "meets a non-innocent woman ... to whom he is sexually and fatally attracted" (quoted in Krutnick, 1991: 137). The existence and aftermath of Dan's "fatal attraction" organizes the film's narrative trajectory (to the point of lending the film its title) and for this many would classify *Fatal Attraction* as a neo-noir, a term generally used to indicate a body of films which self-consciously imitate the styles, tones, and associations popularized in the 1940s versions. Like classic noir, the film externalizes Dan's none-too-innocent desires in its mise en scène, and frames urban settings as places where criminality and hedonism flourish, associations which crystallize in the downtown setting of the meatpacking district, where Alex makes her home. In 1987, this section of Manhattan was culturally abject, and the film visualizes the neighborhood as a nocturnal hell characterized by industrial associations which overwhelm domesticity. Slabs of meat line the streets, workers carry carcasses in the open air, fires burn in abandoned trash canisters, and smoke swirls around the heads of those who ambulate through the night. The sinister connotation speaks to a carnality of desire and the instincts of the flesh, all of which become associated with Alex.[10] (In contrast, Dan resides apparently on the upper East or West Side, a locale that bespeaks sterile wealth. When the family relocates to Westchester, green grass and fall foliage flank the Gallaghers' white, colonial-style home. This pristine setting in turn correlates to Beth, the "good girl," who is overdetermined in her fitness for family life.)

Notably, Dan gives in to Alex and to his extramarital urges in the meatpacking district, and the film's two most graphic love scenes, where the couple copulate beside the kitchen sink and in a freight elevator, take place in this ghettoized locale. The steamy urban setting of the meatpacking district aptly hosts the couple's "crime," so to speak, and Dan and Alex frame their adultery in juridical terms outright. Before the affair transpires they have dinner together in a public restaurant, during which Alex smokes (another telltale sign of the femme fatale) and the conversation eventually treads to the question of whether what they are doing is right. Alex accuses Dan of being "with a strange girl, being a naughty boy." Dan counters with the observation that having dinner together is not a crime, to which Alex replies, "Not yet." But what makes this a crime? If noirs typically concern themselves with actual crimes (most often a plotted murder) Dan's marital transgression appears juvenile by comparison. To consider adultery a crime akin to murder demands recognition of the extent to which Reagan era America demanded fidelity to the family, and to the virtues of house and home. While Dan presumably upholds these values, dutifully caring for and supporting his wife and daughter, twice in the film he makes direct reference to the fact that he doesn't "do family law," and one of these comments is made during his initial dinner with Alex. Thus, one might read Dan's acting out as an expression of his symbolic rejection of the unforgiving demands of fidelity, as exemplified by the fact that, while he might generally be thought to embody the law (he is a lawyer, after all), he nevertheless intentionally and willingly violates those structures that would, among other laws, mandate fidelity.

Dan's job nevertheless confers on him the status as a sort of "everyman," a designation that too coheres with the genre formula for the noir. Williams notes that Douglas is something of a contemporary reincarnation of Fred MacMurray in *Double Indemnity* (1944), the insurance salesman sucked into an erstwhile murder plot (2005: 179). Yet, both Walter Neff and Dan Gallagher have little compunction about becoming embroiled with untoward women, and the rapidity with which Dan decides to partake of an affair highlights that this everyman too possesses a sinister side, akin to the classic noir protagonist who demands little convincing to murder another woman's husband, take on a shady case, or indulge in a suspicious transaction. His impulse to transgress is hardly too deeply repressed; put differently, if the genre highlights the latent desires that protagonists possess but heretofore have not acted upon, Dan identifies himself as precisely such a carrier. All it takes for him to betray a supposedly idealistic marriage is a hiatus from his wife, a rainstorm, and an impromptu dinner. Dan's behavior thereby confirms Frank Krutnik's theorization that the femme fatale "presents the hero with the opportunity to transgress, rather than simply causing his transgression" (1991: 142). Dan's moral ambivalence, in short, makes his affair not only possible but perhaps inevitable.

Only after the affair announces itself as having dire repercussions, in fact, does Dan exhibit guilt over his indiscretion. The story teases audiences with the suggestion that the affair need not have descended into such a morass of violence and recrimination, had Alex simply held up her end of the bargain. This lack of assuredness with regard to Dan's fate represents perhaps the film's most striking departure from noir formula, since noirs typically start after the action has ended (the story imparted via a flashback and narrative voiceover); thus the protagonist's guilt and complicity hang over the story as a silent witness, imparting the ensuing tale with a sense of impending doom. In contrast, Dan's story begins without the weight of any such recrimination, perhaps a testament to the ease with which the affair could have been conducted and forgotten, had Alex not turned vindictive.[11]

The fact that Alex "Forrest" – and here we might note her appellation's associations with the wild – has led or at least accompanied Dan to the dark side registers as well in the film's visual language, specifically in the chiaroscuro lighting that frames the couple's post-coital repose. The camera passes by a boiling coffee pot on the stove, and focuses on an overhead fan, another key noir motif. The fan then siphons the light on and off the couple's faces, as if to visually correlate the temptation of the affair with the alternating swatches of dark and light, which in turn register the division between family life (the "pure" and light) and the extramarital affair (the "immoral" and dark.)[12] This scene also marks the film's investment in noir style, for noirs and many neo-noirs are filmed in black and white, refracting social commentary through visual alternations of light and dark. As was explored in the previous chapter, the characters in this milieu lack a stable moral code and falter in their efforts to resist temptation, a reality that displaces itself onto a black and white palette that organizes the film's costumes, interiors, and lighting. The alternations between dark and light invoke noir themes – deception, greed, and lust – through the recourse they make to its stark visual styles.

If Dan encapsulates the noir's morally ambivalent protagonist, Alex unquestionably functions as the femme fatale, a figure that seduces the hero into the noir world, her feminized appearance a mask for ruthless and masculinized ambition. Alex's status as precisely such a temptress is signaled by her male-sounding first name, "Alex," and by the fact that she organizes the seduction scenes. She is the one who says to Dan over dinner, "We were attracted to each other at the party – that's obvious," a line that indicates the forthright nature with which she enunciates both her desire and Dan's. Alex's designation as a masculinized femme fatale also relies on her difference from the verifiably feminine Beth, a stay-at-home mother who serves as Alex's double/opposite. As Frank Krutnik argues, the hero "is attracted by the woman who sets herself against convention (which is suggested in particular by the presence of the more conventional and loyal good girl, who has either to be rejected by or lost to the hero.) It is then the very danger attached to the femme fatale which makes her desirable to the hero" (1991: 141). Alex's simultaneous separation from, and likeness to, Beth legitimizes her appeal, as does her penchant for exhibitionism and danger. While we have already documented the ways in which sex with Alex identifies itself as an indulgence rather than a responsibility, in the caste of the femme fatale, her sexual proclivities identify her as unscrupulous and immoral. The classic femme fatale uses sex as a means to an end, and here too sex is coded as a self-serving act. While Beth's soft sexuality is clearly put in service of the family, Alex's is not, which again identifies her as the classic femme fatale who employs sex to secure something for herself – in this case, masculine companionship.

Alex's identification as the femme fatale nevertheless begs the question of whether she is an autonomous agent who singlemindedly pursues her own desires, or whether she might be read, as feminist critics have come to posit, as a projection of male fears. The classic noir emerged during and directly following World War II, a time when women had entered the workforce in unprecedented numbers; in the wake of the second-wave feminist movement, the 1980s saw a similar spike in female employment. While the classic noir heroine was a driven woman whose ambitions could often find no socially sanctioned outlet for their expression, Alex's status as a diabolical working woman likewise evidences the promulgation and persistence of fears surrounding women who privilege their own needs and desires over those of men or children. If noirs typically respond to economic anxiety by forging a link between unstable, unsure economies and masculinized, immoral women who take away men's rightful jobs, one way to indulge that suspicion is through stories which vilify such women, thereby blaming them for social ills. As ideological blueprints, noirs ensure that powerful women get the comeuppance they deserve, and in turn provide a cautionary tale for other women who might find their own inclinations trending in directions similar to those of the femme fatale. It is therefore imperative to recognize that Alex's identification as a femme fatale is inextricably linked to her position as a single, professional woman, in that this identity is scapegoated for causing the disappointment she now endures. The film suggests, indeed, that Alex has been left doubly disadvantaged by professional economies which have left her childless and alone at 36, as well as presumably having taught her that violence and aggression are natural routes to rectify that situation.[13]

While the fears of women's entrance into the workforce and the implicit competition they in turn posed to men will be explored in the next chapter, psychoanalytic readings of the femme fatale argue that, rather than take her as a figure in her own right, we might see her appearance as testifying to the male protagonist's own latent insecurities. Joan Copjec argues, for instance, that in order to indemnify himself against the dangers of sexuality, the noir hero treats the femme fatale as his double, to which he surrenders the enjoyment he can not himself sustain (1993: 193). This line of reasoning places the femme fatale in much the same position as the horror "monster" because in both explanatory frameworks Alex emerges as a victim of Dan's disavowed sexual impulses. The subsequent investigation and punishment of Alex thereby identify themselves as Dan's attempts to undo what *he* has done. Consider: Dan breaks into Alex's apartment either searching for evidence that she is either lying about her pregnancy or to find some way to exculpate himself from the burden of fathering an illegitimate child. While the impulse to investigate and punish the femme fatale is a classic noir move, here the punishment and investigation turn on a crime that *Dan* has committed. In the process of this pursuit, Dan surprisingly finds nothing to incriminate Alex further; her pregnancy test seems authentic, and a scrapbook clipping confirms the veracity of her story about her father's unexpected heart attack, although she did attempt to laugh this tale off as a falsehood. If anything, Dan's investigation confirms the legitimacy of what Alex told or tried to tell him – she was traumatized by her father's heart attack, and she is in fact pregnant.

Dan's attempts at revenge also seem to be positioned as retaliations at himself, and as efforts to regain lost control, which supports Elizabeth Cowie's contention that the violent retribution enacted on the femme fatale bears witness to man's attempt to punish the object of desire who has unmanned him (1993: 125). Dan attacks Alex twice, first verbally assaulting her as retribution for having falsely identified herself as a home buyer in order to gain access to his home, and second wordlessly brutalizing her for her illicit kidnapping of Ellen. Although one might argue that Alex "deserves" the punishment that he metes out – Chris Holmlund notes that these attacks are frequently regarded as justifiable, and postulates that middle-class male protagonists tend to get a pass even when attacking women who are physically weaker – in some sense, it is not clear what Dan is hoping to achieve (1994: 141–2). He apparently wants to scare Alex into submission, to convince her to leave him alone.[14] But, the difficulty of reading the attack scene as a triumph of masculinity is that it still fingers Dan as the one who lacks control. While raging against Alex, his fear and anxiety register more palpably than do hers; he chases her around the apartment, but then capitulates when granted the chance to actually kill her. By contrast, when Alex attacks him with a knife, she appears intent on killing him, and does not do so only because he wrenches the knife away from her. Here, the ineffectual protagonist lashes out in a shamed response to his own sexual impulses, but finds himself spectacularly unable to overcome his symbolic castration. Again, we might contrast Dan's paralysis in this scene to the fact that Alex is a far more effective agent of home invasion than is he. While his intrusions end rather futilely, Alex's, by contrast, achieve their implied goal; she succeeds in tricking Beth into giving her an unlisted phone number, kills the bunny, and almost kills Beth.

As Alex's many successes confirm, the danger of the femme fatale is in some ways her unflappability, which emerges in direct contrast to Dan's fear and shame. While she is not a cool, calculating femme fatale who makes no mistakes, Alex's control of the situation outmatches Dan's in almost every instance – she steamrolls the affair, shows up in his office, and infiltrates his home multiple times. In this way, the femme fatale's presence inadvertently reveals the instability of male power; while Alex acts on her own behalf, Dan's moves are constantly defensive and reactive. Though audiences are encouraged to regard Alex as the figure who rouses Dan's desire and deserves eradication, the film nevertheless paradoxically points to the insecurity of the masculine ethos.

Seduction and Danger in the Erotic Thriller

While *Fatal Attraction*'s storylines and iconic character types comply in many ways with the classic noir, its marriage of graphic sex and imminent danger catapult *Fatal Attraction* into the category of the erotic thriller.[15] As Linda Ruth Williams argues, erotic thrillers distinguish themselves from noir by the fact that erotic thrillers read "sex as crime" and privilege or foreground sex over narrative (2005: 36). Such a definition coheres with *Fatal Attraction*'s insistence on depicting intense bodily pleasure; confirming its status as an erotic thriller is the fact that it too operates at the apex of noir and porn. This attribution is perhaps most evident in the steamy "elevator scene," where Alex forcefully takes Dan into the elevator and aggressively closes the heavy grates behind them. Once inside, the couple are framed by the grate's vertical lines, which look like prison bars. These images of entrapment as well as the focus on bare lightbulbs, a massive overhead light, and dramatic overhead shots deliberately invoke noir; at the same time, the exposure of Alex's bare breast and her oral pleasuring of Dan mark the scene as pornographic.

As the elevator scene displays, in the erotic thriller the thrills are *in* the sex, or the sex drives the thriller; as David Andrews argues, in the erotic thriller "sex is dangerous" (2006: 59). Confirming this, the elevator scene contains the threat of exposure: Alex purposefully stops the open-air elevator between floors, and Dan watches in a paralyzed fashion as a man walks above the shaft. The look on Dan's face borders on excruciation – Dan winces between pleasure and pain since the couple are about to be exposed in flagrante. This marriage of sex and danger presents itself as the erotic thriller's key thematic motif. Moreover, while sex is the crime, it portends greater violations, since graphic sexual expression ends or threatens to end in murder, in this case, in the murder of the femme fatale. In this, however, the film departs somewhat from the genre formula. Writing about what he calls the "thriller of murderous passions," Charles Derry notes that it is typically the "adulterous lovers who, sinfully and coldbloodedly, kill the hapless spouse; in *Fatal Attraction*, it is the marriage partners who savagely and in concert kill the adulterous *outsider*" (2001: 102). The flipping of this formula is particularly interesting in light of the film's historical context, since the film could not reconstitute the nuclear family unless both spouses are kept alive. Thus, Alex's death reads as a reinstatement of a preferred world wherein the family triumphs.

More so than any other genre term described here, the designation of the erotic thriller best accounts for *Fatal Attraction*'s embodied nature. Erotic and thriller are terms of response, Linda Ruth Williams reminds us, and the erotic thriller should thrill its viewers through "narrative suspense and engagement, and through sexual delivery"; she adds, erotic thrillers promise that audiences "will be erotically thrilled as well as criminally thrilled" (2005: 25). Likewise highlighting audience anticipation and reward as a defining feature of the genre, David Andrews argues that "the genre promises a dual spectacle: sexual action and violent suspense" (2006: 59). While *Fatal Attraction*'s two graphic sex scenes deliver on the promise of erotic thrills through their repeated emphasis on the naked body, audience participation is also solicited in later scenes which are thrilling, suspenseful, or scary. This organizational structure, whereby the film indulges prurient interests early by showcasing its graphic sex scenes in the first half hour and then turns to suspense and violence, involves audiences in the sexual act, priming them for the similarly visceral danger that follows; as Andrews writes, the sexual spectacle "serves as a prelude to a more extensive pattern of rage escalating into violence" (2006: 64).

The film uses the intense reactions solicited by the sex to prepare audiences for analogously intense bodily responses of terror or fear, responses again propelled by Alex. While Alex is the initial source of erotic interest (and the primary visual object of the sex scenes), she soon transmogrifies into the film's foremost agent of pain infliction. The erotic thriller operates primarily according to a corporeal logic, since its main methodology for processing and understanding events derives from their incitement of either pleasure or pain, and the genre organizes itself around the suggestion that the two are roundly indistinguishable. The roller coaster scene is particularly self-referential in this regard, crosscutting as it does between Alex's and Ellen's exhilarating ride and Beth's frantic car sequence. Notably, this scene might be understood as an update of the "cinema of attractions," a term used to refer to the way that cinema was a medium initially intended to shock and thrill spectators. Locating the roller coaster as a visual correlative for the experience of movie-going, Linda Williams has argued that the roller coaster analogy is apt, because in both experiences thrills are produced through an unprecedented experience of disorientation, destabilization, and terror (2000: 358). The roller coaster ride thereby provides a correlative not only for the way Alex, Ellen, and Beth feel, but also for audience response. It is difficult to determine, for instance, whether Alex and Ellen are screaming in terror or in pleasure, and in fact, the scene would suggest both, for such commixture is precisely the reason the roller coaster is such a popular experience. This roller coaster concept of film viewing invites audiences to enjoy the sensation of feeling threatened and out of control.

The simultaneity of pleasure and terror organizes a number of the film's subsequent scenes, and another unique pleasure of the erotic thriller is the surprise attack that is not entirely a surprise. While Alex's appearance in the mirror behind Beth is gasp-inducing, as is the moment when an undead Alex rises up out of her watery grave, audiences are nevertheless by this point trained to regard the appearance of Alex with shock and fear, and to take seriously her determination to wreak havoc. Likewise, although the Gallagher family appears ensconced in their cozy home during the prelude to Alex's attack, audiences know not to trust that sense of security; instead, the thriller formula dictates that an attack is imminent, and the only aspect left to chance is how or when it will occur. The nearness of death for Dan, Alex, and Beth at almost all times confirms the danger instigated by the sexual act, and the specific nature of this peril is explored further in Chapter Four. That the film begins in pleasure and ends in terror, however, confirms its affinity with a genre in which thrills arise from the coterminous nature of pleasure and pain.

Fatal Attraction's status as an ur-text for the erotic thriller has been asserted by various critics, many of whom note the impact of the film on subsequent offerings which code illicit sexuality as deadly. To enjoy this position as an inaugural text and deem itself worthy of mimicry, however, *Fatal Attraction* first had to establish its commercial appeal. Notably, the massive popularity of the film was dependent in part on a word-of-mouth campaign that enjoyed unprecedented success. The garnering of such enthusiasm, however, must be understood as resulting not simply from the fact that the film effectively hybrized genres, or borrowed from recognizable iconography. Instead, the film clearly had its finger on the pulse of American politics and social concerns, a prescience which also made it a lightning rod for controversy about the status of feminism, working women, and male entitlement. The next chapter contextualizes the film within its historical moment with an eye to explicating the film's polarizing entry in the American culture wars.

Chapter 3

Career Women of the 1980s:
Feminism and the Reception History of *Fatal Attraction*

As messages go, this ain't subtle. Fatal Attraction *tells married men to stop fooling around or risk bringing the house down. It lashes unmarried career women for having made the wrong choice, and it tells them to marry lest they go nuts. And it tells everyone that female desire is demanding, ensnaring – in short, it will swallow up your life.*
(Marcia Pally, "Kin Con: The Family Goes Bananas", p.12)

Shortly after *Fatal Attraction*'s release on September 18, 1987, a bevy of criticism emerged about the film's anti-feminist tendencies, much of which pointed out the questionable politics that informed the presentation of a working woman so unsatisfied with her singlehood that she is willing to kill to put an end to it. As Susan Bromley and Pamela Hewitt declare, "The unflinching message of *Fatal Attraction* is that women who opt for the career track are to be viewed not merely as unfeminine, but also as destructive who must be themselves destroyed" (1992: 17). Or, as Lydia Sargent pessimistically wrote, "This movie has put the final nail in the coffin of an already-dying women's lib movement" (1988: 34). As these comments indicate, *Fatal Attraction* cleaved an American culture that had already witnessed a much-touted decline in feminist sentiments, a place where women's roles were rapidly changing and thus a major source of cultural tension, a moment, in the terms set forth by Susan Faludi, of feminist "backlash." This chapter takes up the reception history of the film from the perspective of feminism, engaging with *Fatal Attraction*'s rebuke to single working women as well as its timeliness, since its release coincided with the publication of a high-profile *Newsweek* article which stated that a single 40-year-old woman had a better chance of being killed by a terrorist than getting married.

Because *Fatal Attraction* emerged during a time period wherein middle-class women's entry in the labor market was greeted with suspicion if not outright disdain, the film's portrayal of Alex as a homicidal career woman hungrily seeking not only masculine companionship but also a child rankled many feminists. As they suggested, Alex's life of financial independence and sexual freedom is cast not as a feminist dream, but rather as a nightmare of regret and worry, a representation which betrays the threat that non-normative women pose to patriarchal structures. As a cautionary figure, Alex appears as a woman who has clearly paid too high a price for her independence, and many believed that turning a successful female professional into a psychotic killer indicated the film's disdain for women who stray from conventional feminine roles. Accordingly, feminists charged that Alex was not so much a villain in her own right as the product or symptom of a larger cultural context riddled with anxieties over the status of single, working women. This chapter focuses on these debates, paying particular attention to the ways that the film was apprehended as symptomatic of waning feminist sentiments and ideals in American culture at large. Included in this analysis will be a consideration of Michael Douglas' star image as an "everyman" terrorized by a vindictive career woman, and a discussion of the film's alternate ending, one that was soundly rejected by test audiences because it failed to "punish" Alex enough.

"Kill the Bitch"

A widely repeated story surrounding *Fatal Attraction*'s release in the popular marketplace features scores of impassioned American filmgoers sitting in darkened theaters, yelling at the screen in anger and rage, "Kill the bitch!"[1] The specter of a vituperative American public eager to hasten Alex's imminent death has become a highly mythologized aspect of the film text itself; some twenty years out, it is difficult to think about the film except as one where Alex's death is both overdetermined and justified. In part, this viewpoint has been established because the film is enunciated through Dan's perspective – he is the central narrative agent, and audiences are privy to his viewpoint virtually throughout. Clearly, then, it is Alex's threat to Dan (and his even more innocent family) that audiences seek to eradicate. Yet, "Kill the bitch" is likewise a demand for blood lust, a sentiment so strong that it is worth asking why the figure of Alex garnered such an unforgiving response, and why, indeed, indulging that need for revenge was so pleasurable for the audiences who came to see the film in droves.

To answer this question, we might turn first to the historical context of Reagan era America in the 1980s, a culture that was becoming increasingly inhospitable to feminist ideals. Thanks in part to the emergence of America's New Right, the moral majority, the rise in religious fundamentalism, and an individualist thrust in social policy now commonly referred to as neoconservatism, the culture pendulum swung in support of a return to "family values," sentiments that were assumed to have been assaulted by leftist cultural movements in previous eras. Under this new paradigm, the nuclear family reemerged as the repository for all morality, and was touted as the solution to cultural and social ills. That American culture was being urged to reprioritize the family was evidenced in political as well as social discourse; as media scholar Daniel Marcus has argued, Reagan advocated a nostalgic return to family stability by citing idealized images of the 1950s which he then encouraged the 1980s populace to emulate.

Such a return to core values involved an embrace of stereotypical female roles, and women were urged to willingly choose domestic identities and reposition motherhood as their prima facie accomplishment. (While the sentiments preexisted the terminology, the apt term "new traditionalism" was codified to describe this trend, and stems from a 1988 ad campaign in *Good Housekeeping* magazine featuring pictures of women at home, as they proclaimed the satisfactions of wifehood and motherhood.) Yet, at the same time that women were being told that they belonged at home, actual women were increasingly delaying marriage and childbearing, as well as securing employment in unprecedented numbers. According to the U.S. Census

Bureau, in 1965, 36.7 percent of the labor force was comprised of adult women; by 1987, those figures rose to 55.4 percent (quoted in Berland and Wechter, 1992: 39). While these were considered feminist gains by many, women who failed to adhere to conventional standards also found themselves at the receiving end of a cultural barrage which encouraged them to look with anxiety at the domestic opportunities they were likewise squandering.

Women who did not embody the new traditionalist ideal were assaulted by the message that they were in danger of precluding their chances for happiness, as they risked never getting married or having children. Implicit in this sentiment, which Susan Faludi famously named the "backlash," was the idea that feminism had done women wrong because it limited rather than expanded their life choices. According to such ideology, women's vaunted equality had left them lonely and miserable, and their so-called liberation was actually a harness because it denied them access to feminine pleasures. (Faludi smartly contended that gender equality was never in fact realized in America, but that it encroached enough to make the patriarchy nervous.) Perhaps the best-known iteration of this backlash as a caution to female ambition came in the form of *Newsweek*'s much-touted article predicting the shrinking chances of matrimony for women over the age of 30; statistics reported that by age 35 the probability of a woman marrying dropped to 5 percent, and by 40, "a woman was more likely to be killed by a terrorist than to marry."[2] Such sentiments frame marriage and childbearing as experiences with self-evident rewards, and see such benefits as outweighing any satisfactions that might be provided by work or professional economies. Situating normative familial identities as women's foremost desire, articles such as these encouraged single women to scrutinize their personal lives for signs that they too could be a statistical casualty, and warned that women who do not marry preclude what amounts to their only chance at happiness.

Fatal Attraction frames the issue in similar terms, and parrots this marriage and maternal panic most famously when Alex comments that she is planning to keep her and Dan's baby, because "I'm 36 years old, it may be my last chance to have a child." Dogged by the knowledge that "time is running out," Alex acts in accordance with a popular mentality keen on reminding women that, once they are past 30, time is not on their side as it concerns marriage and children.[3] Referencing such pressures, Faludi quotes an industry insider who speculates that the film is a "psychotic manifestation of the marriage study reported in *Newsweek* – the one predicting that single women over 30 were doomed to spinsterhood" (1988: 50). If we read the film as one addressed to single women, *Fatal Attraction* cautions them what *not* to do, lest they want to end up coveting other people's families (and, the film implies, boiling bunnies). As Laurie Stone wrote in *Ms.*, the film "says that good women stay home … while single working women are damaged, barely even human, and want to destroy the family they also secretly covet" (1987: 79). In the culture war over female roles, the stay-at-home mother rebukes the single one for ignoring the fact that the most fulfilling life comes from living in harmony with traditional familial ideals.

In this unforgiving paradigm, it is assumed that women who place career or other considerations above the domestic will not merely regret the choice, but may even find their sanity challenged. As Lydia Sargent quipped,

> The message is clear, gals. Accept it. Act on it. Any gal who gets to be thirty-six years old and has a career, a photo album of her dead father, no mother to speak of, an opera collection, a loft apartment in a seedy neighborhood, and a large freight elevator INSTEAD of a loving husband, a dog, a cute daughter, a country home, a good cookbook, a Volvo, and a bunny rabbit, is completely PSYCHOTIC. (1988: 35)

Though Sargent's rhetoric is deliberately inflammatory, good evidence exists to support the idea that the film aligns female loneliness with mental instability, and even scripts them as causally related. The first real clue to Alex's psychosis occurs, for instance, on the Sunday night when Dan tries to leave her apartment and return home. She claws at his shirt, beats him, and slits her wrists, all drastic and violent actions designed to coerce his presence and attention. Likewise, after Alex meets Beth in the guise of a prospective house buyer, Dan comes over to Alex's apartment and tells her this has to stop. Alex initially demands his respect, reminding him she is the mother of his child. Yet, when he motions to leave, she again goes crazy, pleading, "Please don't go, I didn't mean it."

The portrayal of Alex as a woman suddenly desperate for attention because she has no one in her life save Dan is somewhat inconsistent with the previous presentation of her character, since Alex appears initially as a woman with a high-powered career and a presumably active life. Yet, the film quickly distances itself from this initial attribution, making it clear that it has instrumentalized Alex's job as an excuse for her chance meeting with Dan. Indeed, subsequent to Dan's and Alex's first two meetings (at the book party and business meeting respectively), audiences hear nothing more about Alex's position as an editor, nor does Alex appear to have any other familial or social outlets. As Sandra Joshel writes: "Her independence becomes isolation: she sees no friends, colleagues, or relations. Having established her as a woman without a man, the film inverts its own logic and reinscribes her as a woman whose life is totally engaged with one, so that we see and hear her voice only in relation to Dan" (1992: 60). The suggestion that Alex has no other personal relationships save for this one – while Beth, by contrast, exists in a warm social cocoon populated not only by her husband and child, but also by their friends and her parents – clearly privileges the married woman's life over that of the single career woman. As well, the notion that familial ties ensure a life replete with love and companionship provides the explanatory framework for the singlemindedness with which Alex approaches her relation with Dan, for it suggests that occupying the role of wife and mother provides access to a large social network.

In the film's formulation, Alex's behaviors are rationalized by the desire both to be like Beth, and to have what Beth has. The cruel mix of isolation and envy that characterizes her life apparently leads Alex to a peculiar form of identity theft, whereby many of Alex's most psychotic behaviors can be explained as attempts to secure for herself the privileges and pleasures of family life. Alex cooks Dan dinner, as a traditional wife would, and then, in perverse recodification of that action, cooks the bunny; her invitation to Dan that he accompany her to a performance of *Madame Butterfly* perhaps hopes to capitalize on

The triangulated relations of Beth, Alex, and Dan are here encapsulated in the scene's blocking.

the kind of "standing date" that spouses enjoy; and finally, her afternoon spent with Beth in the family condominium allows her to pass time as Beth presumably does, drinking tea as she awaits Dan's arrival home from work. The most obvious of such attempts at usurpation is of course Alex's kidnapping of Ellen, an action which affords Alex the opportunity to mimic Beth's position as a maternal presence at least for one afternoon. The crosscutting sequence frames Alex's maternal impulse as an impulse to be like Beth, who is at once her rival and her ideal. Alex's multiple attempts to inhabit Beth's life also become uniquely literalized when Alex appears in the Gallaghers' bathroom at the end of the film, when Alex tells Beth that she is "stupid" and asks Beth what Beth is doing in *her* house, clearly operating under the delusion that she is Dan's wife and Beth constitutes the intruder. While this transposition is of course meant to underscore the completeness of Alex's psychic break, it too showcases the extent to which the film comes down to a battle of femininities whereby the working, single woman is so consumed by the thought of the family she does not have that she creates a fictionalized version of her life wherein she does.[4]

According to the film's logic, singlehood ushers in unhappiness and loneliness, whereas the contented image of Beth counters the presentation of Alex as a woman who refuses to face the punishing effects of her own choices. Unlike Alex, Beth seems to have avoided being haunted by "what if" questions; untroubled by her station, Beth's life is spent happily tending to her daughter, preparing for social engagements with her friends, relaxing in the country with her parents, and painting and decorating her new house. According to Liahna Babener, Beth makes "wifely accommodation a hallmark of the marriage," and Babener likewise notes that Beth accepts the primacy of Dan's career without complaint, allowing him the weekend in the city without recrimination, and even suggesting that there is food in the refrigerator for him to eat (1992: 27). As such a model of wifely solicitude, Beth also solicits both the desiring gaze of Dan and the camera: she is sensual and seems sexually available, even if the requirements of domesticity and socialization frequently get in the way of the couple's intimacy. Such visual and thematic glorifications of Beth frame her life as comfortable and happy, and endorse feminine identities that adhere to traditional gender standards. Indeed, the film offers no indication that Beth is anything like the disillusioned housewives invoked in numerous feminist tracts, most notably Betty Friedan's *The Feminine Mystique*. While Friedan lamented the constrictions imposed by stifling domestic roles, Beth's life appears, conversely, as if filled with all the love, companionship, and excitement for which she could ever hope.[5]

While much has been made of the fact that Alex's single status informs her despair, it is crucial to note that Alex is also a single *working* woman and that as such, she apparently has only herself to blame for her fate because she has been working away the years while her biological clock is ticking. This unflattering characterization of Alex as a working woman rather than a maternal figure complies in significant ways with the 1980s cultural zeitgeist, and the Reagan era is now routinely understood as one which tended to scapegoat the breakdown of the family, and in turn working women, for social ills. Lacking satisfying explanation for dramatic declines in economic markets and, in turn, job prospects and opportunities, Reagan, for instance, blamed the sluggish economy of the early 1980s on the entry of women into the workforce. In a speech in 1982, Reagan noted that unemployment was due not so much to recession as to the "great increase of the people going into the job market, and – ladies, I'm not picking on anyone, but ..." (quoted in Faludi, 1991: 67).[6] As such comments indicate, the hostility toward the influx of women into the work force stemmed from real anxieties about cultural competition and declining financial prospects – the economically devastating Black Monday (in which the largest one-day percentage decline in stock market history took place) occurred on October 19, 1987, about a month after *Fatal Attraction*'s release, and thus coincided with the height of its popularity.

In myriad ways, the weight of social scrutiny fell upon the working woman during the 1980s; in addition to being implicated in economic downturns, she bore blame for having exacerbated myriad social ills including America's shifting standards of living, the breakdown of families, infidelity, incompetent parenting, rising abortion rates, and increased instances of divorce. Insofar as it scripts a career woman who tempts Dan into an affair, using adultery to render vulnerable the much-beloved nuclear family, *Fatal Attraction* would appear to side with those who believe that working women threaten domestic stability. As well, Alex seems to actively desire the destruction of a family for selfish ends. By coding Alex as self-serving and maniacal, the film showcased and combated the assault she makes on imperiled "family values," the vaunted set of sentiments held to be the only salvation for a nation in crisis. If reconstituting the family in the face of economic and social insecurity was one of the nation's foremost preoccupations in the late 1980s, Alex's bloody death serves as a powerful wish fulfillment.

While *Fatal Attraction*'s conservative endorsements of the importance of the family were seen as a counter to the forces of social degeneration perpetrated by independent women like Alex, the film's misogynistic tendencies were also directly attributed to its director, Adrian Lyne. Lyne, who began as a director of commercials, was already known in Hollywood for films like *Flashdance* (1983) and *9½ Weeks* (1986), both of which blatantly sexualize their female leads and take pleasure in spectacles of female subjugation. *Fatal Attraction*'s graphic sex scenes demonstrated consistency within Lyne's oeuvre, but, more importantly, Lyne's publicly derisive views of working women were thought to influence the film's positioning of Alex. Faludi in particular took Lyne to task for statements which indicated that he found working women's lives to be lonely and unfulfilled, and she quotes Lyne at length on his dislike of powerful women ("they are sort of overcompensating for not being men"); his conviction that women who achieve equality will find it empty ("sure you got your career and success, but you are not fulfilled as a woman"); and his repugnance at overly sexual women ("it's kind of unattractive, however liberated and emancipated it is"). Faludi also quotes actor Michael Douglas on his sympathy for men who have been the undeserving targets of the feminist movement ("guys are going through a terrible crisis right now because of women's unreasonable demands") (1991: 121). In Faludi's feminist reading, Lyne's and Douglas' belief that working women sacrifice their femininity saturates *Fatal Attraction*, and in turn, the film justifies a male gaze which looks at such women with suspicion and hostility. This last quote, where Douglas professes sympathy for male "victims" suffering at the hands of overbearing women, is particularly significant in this regard, because in many respects *Fatal Attraction* is far less a story about a powerful, professional woman than a tale about what a powerful professional woman does *to* a man.

The hostility with which the film's director and its premiere male star view working women and, in turn, feminism, suggests that strong women in the film are recast through the eyes of men, a perspective that helps to explain the film's vilification of women who are coded as holding feminist views. As Joshel writes, the film constructs a "feminism" which it robs of authority, "by showing it to be a cover for women's manipulation or punishment of men" (1992: 61). In keeping with an ethos ever attuned to the ways that feminism endangers men, the film frames all of Alex's supposed liberations not as freedoms but rather as lies, since she pretends to postures of autonomy and independence that she does not actually feel. In fact, despite giving lip service to the fact that she "hates it" when men ogle her, later saying that what she really wants from Dan is "respect," what Alex really wants is companionship, and she retaliates vindictively at its denial. As well, her pregnancy serves the purpose of commandeering Dan's repeated attention; as Joshel writes, "'feminist' rhetoric is employed to disallow the man's denials of relationship and marshalled to hold onto him. The demand that Dan uphold his responsibilities for their child becomes a demand that he remain in her life. Throughout, feminist words are connected with Alex's delusions about the relationship" (1992: 61). While the insistence that Dan acknowledge his responsibilities is not wholly preposterous, the film nevertheless positions this as a false posture which sets out to get men by the jugular, thereby revealing feminist ideals not as justifiable demands for equality or fair treatment, but rather as the ravings of a needy, deluded woman.

Though even the law would mandate that Dan acknowledge his parental responsibility, when this assertion emerges from Alex, it is undercut and invalidated as a tactical maneuver designed primarily to disrupt Dan's life. As explored in Chapter Four, Alex's desire to carry the pregnancy to term is framed as an assault on him, rather than her right. Dan claims that Alex's decision to keep the baby is her choice, and "has nothing to do with me," even though this statement is patently false. Yet, rather than expose it as such, the film scripts Alex as the one in error, since her increasingly diabolical efforts to be noticed by Dan read as proof that she is losing her grip on reality. Babener writes, "given the compulsive cast of her own behavior and the extremity of her charges, standard feminist grievances are thus discredited as the raving of a demented person, and the character made to stand for the feminist voice is constructed as an odious exemplar" (1992: 30). The gesture of putting feminist demands in the mouth of a woman whom the film so clearly despises makes feminism and its belief systems seem at once ridiculous, cunning, manipulative, sneaky, greedy, and mendacious, thereby scripting the movement in precisely the terms that the director and his actor regard it – as an unreasonable assault on unsuspecting men.

The alignment of Alex's statements with feminist edicts script Alex as the token feminist, yet everything that she does in the name of this paradigm only proves its fallibility. As well, because this parable focuses on what feminism does to men, rather than, say, what feminism is, it advocates most strongly on behalf of undeserving men burdened with excessive female demands. Actively worrying over the men consumed in a torrent of female wrath, the film validates the standard caricature of the angry feminist whose *raison d'être* is furious retaliation at any cost. Alex's rage is indeed her scariest feature, for Dan faces a woman whose emotional reach apparently knows no boundaries, one willing to go to increasingly outlandish extremes to ensure that the wrongs committed against her receive a public airing. As Ellen Willis observes, "the real irony of *Fatal Attraction* is that it has less to do with lust or love or infidelity than with a man's panicky craving for shelter from the storm of female rage" (1987: 86).[7] While Alex's rage is eloquently reiterated, it is nevertheless given very little justification. As Elaine Berland and Marilyn Wechter note: "The film narrative offers no plausible reason for her alternating current of seductiveness and rage. There is no evidence presented to support a break from the woman originally seen as a competent, attractive professional to the woman shown as disheveled and out of control" (1992: 41). The film delegitimizes this break, in turn, by refusing to adequately narrate the transition that Alex makes from successful woman to enraged lunatic.

The film does spend considerable time, however, establishing the effect of Alex's rage on Dan. It makes this point by emphasizing that Alex's anger is a demanding, one-sided pursuit, an observation best exemplified in the scene where she follows him home to his country house, where she appears as a haunting, predatory presence. Dressed in black, Alex watches surreptitiously from above as Dan travels in an open-air elevator in the parking garage, carrying the bunny, and arrives at his waiting car, which she has drenched with acid. When Dan, now in a rental car, leaves the garage Alex secretly begins following behind, and he begins playing her tape, which was delivered to his office earlier that day. The scene crosscuts between shots of each of them driving, and the tape provides a sound bridge over both of their countenances, as Dan gets increasingly more aggrieved. The tape begins with Alex's invocation of the interpenetration of their two bodies, suggestively reminding Dan that "a part of you is growing inside of me." As if to underscore her succubus-like presence, Alex reiterates: "I feel you, I taste you, I think you, I touch you." This dialogue visibly disgusts Dan, as evidenced by his tortured expression and his anxiety as he runs his fingers through his hair. This scene also nicely spatializes the notion of penetration, for Alex's words penetrate the supposedly safe cocoon of his car, submerging Dan. As Naomi Segal writes, "In this traditionally penetrative fantasy of sexual irruption, the subject of forced entry is female and familial: she enters more insistently because she is an already containing unit, herself both penetrated by and penetrative of the man's psychological space" (1997: 204).

Alex's taped content quickly turns from a sexually laden dialogue to a diatribe reminding Dan of his responsibilities; she accuses him of thinking of no one but himself, and criticizes him for finding her demands so "unreasonable." (In this, she parrots *his* earlier language, when he told her to be reasonable, since she "knew the rules.") Alex's verbal lashing continues with her calling Dan a "cock-sucking son of a bitch," and she subsequently offers an accusation obviously meant as an insult to his masculinity: "I bet you don't even like girls, do you?" Alex's mood shift from desperate devotion to principled accusation to verbal abuse culminates in her final conclusion (which Dan listens to later than night) that Dan is afraid of her. She says, "You're afraid of me, aren't you, you gutless, heartless, spineless son of a bitch?" While Alex is probably not wrong – Dan *is* afraid of her – the accusation castrates Dan, since it points out his multiple failings, not the least of which is his failure to successfully contain her. As if to emphasize Dan's inability to neutralize Alex, the next scene shows him visiting a police station in the name of a "friend" who is being terrorized by an irrational woman. The police officer mocks Dan, telling him that there is little they can do until Dan catches her doing something overt, adding: "It's his bed, he's going to have to lie in it."

The logic which underpins the driving sequence, and indeed the logic which feminists found fault with in the film as a whole, stems from its assignment of deviancy to a desirous women, to its sense that when women want things that desire inevitably gets out of control. As film critic Pauline Kael incisively noted, "This shrewd film also touches on something deeper than men's fear of feminism: their fear of women, their fear of women's emotions, of women's hanging on to them" (1987: 106). This masculinist perspective assaults feminism's core belief that women and men deserve the same opportunities; in *Fatal Attraction*, that belief is redressed to show that, if given the same opportunities, women will flail around miserably because they are less equipped than men to exercise their choices or freedoms. Made crazy by, apparently, having made choices that in turn lead to disappointments, Alex's stalking presence reminds us that female desires can turn all-encompassing, excessive and over the top.

A feminist critique in turn points out the double standard at work in such a formulation, for certainly the men in *Fatal Attraction* are afforded sexual *and* professional lives, and are not asked, as the women in this film are, to choose between their personal lives and their jobs. What is taken for granted for men seems to be the pivot on which female lives turn, for Alex's lack of connection to the social order has presumably been precluded by her working, whereas Beth's connections are ensured because she does not. The female characters clearly bear the brunt of this unequal system: even if the film seems to take every opportunity to emphasize Dan's impotence, Dan is still a man with innumerable privileges and accesses, privileges denied to the women in the film. Feminist logic demands then that the obvious be stated: despite all the ways that Dan "suffers," institutionalized patriarchy still buttresses his position in the social order and insists on the restoration of his family to him.

The naturalization of such a double standard also serves as an explanatory framework for why audiences were so willing to forgive Dan, but demanded vengeance on Alex. Foisting blame for the affair on the single woman who presumably betrays no one when she embarks on this fling, unlike Dan who betrays everyone, the film nevertheless suggests that, because Alex possesses no redeeming qualities, she deserves to suffer and die. The pleasure of watching Alex get her comeuppance therefore derives in part from the fact that the film offers audiences no reason to desire her exoneration, while it offers many justifications in favor of Dan's. As the next section will discuss, Dan's status as an "everyman" works in tandem with this dynamic in that it earns sympathy for him and dialogues intertextually with Michael Douglas' star image as a man repeatedly and unfairly victimized by powerful women.

The Everyman and the Career Woman

In the promotional documentary shot for *Fatal Attraction*'s 15th anniversary, Michael Douglas explains that he was best able to get into character after observing that there is an "archetypal quality" to Dan Gallagher. Douglas describes a thought process wherein he realized that, "I could be a lawyer in New York City, I could possibly have had an affair, and this nightmare could have happened to me." Dan's attribution as an "everyman" who made a fatal mistake was in fact key to his appeal because, as *Fatal Attraction*'s producers admitted, one of the steepest challenges they faced in getting the film made was that they had to make Dan sympathetic, even though this is a film about a family man who cheats on his wife within the first fifteen minutes of the action.[8] Dan's likeability and hence the film's success hinged on its ability to believably portray Dan as an ordinary person suddenly thrust into dramatically extraordinary circumstances. As Lyne explains, "you are one of them. You are Glenn or Michael. You're normal, but if pushed ... who knows? The situation in this movie is fairly routine. A man has a brief affair, and then the woman becomes a crazed beast. It could happen to anyone" (Hirschberg, 1987: 14).[9] What is perhaps extraordinary about *Fatal Attraction* is how well that message of "ordinariness" translated to the screen, since audiences refused to lambast Dan as a cheating cad, but rather understood him as a man undeserving of the calamity that befalls him. The *National Review*'s John Simon testifies to the film's successful interpellation of spectators on this level, writing in a review that, "This can happen to any married man, as profuse sympathetic male groans in the audience seemed to attest" (1987: 57).

The narrative thus multiply overdetermines the message that audiences should regard Dan not as an unsympathetic philanderer but rather as an amiable husband tortured by one mistake, an attribution anchored by the fact that Dan does not seek out his affair. Instead, he stumbles into it through a series of incidental coincidences, including Alex's presence at his Saturday-morning business meeting, the ensuing rainstorm, his faulty umbrella, and his and Alex's decision to wait out the storm in a nearby restaurant. As well, their affair is apparently Dan's first extramarital offense, and Alex is generally the sexual pursuer – she physically pushes him into her building, and Dan's obvious sexual nervousness is evidenced by the fact that he says "thank god" following Alex's first compliment of his prowess. As well, Alex insists they spend another day and night together after their initial Saturday-night foray, even resorting to a manipulative suicide attempt in order to coerce his presence. Likewise, Dan's concern for his family in the wake of the affair (if not during it) establishes Dan's likeability, and he exhibits demonstrable remorse when he realizes that he has unwittingly jeopardized his wife and child, especially when he visits Beth at her hospital room following her car accident and sits by her bedside in tears. As he divulges to his friend while confessing his affair, "I don't want to lose my family." While the film then offers a sometimes conflicted picture of the constrictions imposed by family life, on this point it is unequivocal: subsequent to realizing that Alex intends to derail his life in every way possible, Dan wants nothing more than to forget that his indiscretion ever took place.

Dan's worth is an estimate achieved at the expense of Alex, since the more psychotic she appears, the more humanized he is. In this, the two characters seem to relate to each other by inverse proportionality: the angrier Alex gets, the less she seems like a victim, and, in turn, the more Dan appears to be one. As Joyce Thompson argues: "It is not sufficient that the hero be likable, his seducer must be made reprehensible. The more ideal the family Alex violates, the more repugnant she is" (1992: 8). Deriving pathos from the fact that Dan is outmatched by Alex's rage and by her cunning intelligence, the film encourages the estimation that Dan does not bear responsibility for the calamities that befall him. According to such logic, Dan's downfall happens at the hands of a powerful, angry woman who disadvantages him at every turn.

As an ideological blueprint, Dan's status as a victim of female wrath rather than an agent of his own destiny complies as well with a cultural moment fixated on questioning what women's increasing cultural and economic independence meant to men, and, thanks largely to his role in *Fatal Attraction*, Michael Douglas became the prototype figure for the "outmatched male." This portrayal represents something of an intensification and recodification of the more desperate or over-the-top qualities of Douglas' star image in the early 1980s, for prior to his casting as Dan, Douglas occupied roles where masculinity was embattled but ultimately triumphant, as exemplified by his status as action hero/adventurer Jack Colton in *Romancing the Stone* (1984) and *Jewel of the Nile* (1985). Similarly, Douglas' maniacal Gordon Gekko in *Wall Street* (1987) became a metonymic figure for corporate pillaging ("greed is good") thanks to his take-no-prisoners approach to the vagaries of economic manipulation. However, one might argue that the over-the-top quality of Douglas' turns as an action hero and as a corporate mogul inadvertently points out the heights that masculinity must scale to retain its vaunted omnipotence.

The tipping point for Douglas' transition from powerful to overpowered can perhaps best be seen in his portrayal of Oliver Rose, the materially successful and embittered husband in *War of the Roses* (1989), where he engages in both subversive manipulation and knockdown, drag-out battles with soon-to-be-ex-wife Barbara (Kathleen Turner). Because Turner was also his love interest in the *Romancing the Stone* franchise, *War of the Roses* provided an intertextual and ironic addendum to that relationship. In this post-romance black comedy, the two play a feuding couple whose divorce leads them to increasingly egregious acts of violence against each other and the eventual annihilation of their shared abode. The characterization of Douglas as slightly outmatched by his vindictive wife left him well poised for the attributions of male victimization that would later dominate his career.

War of the Roses presciently begot Douglas as one who could codify the battle of the sexes for mass audiences. This ability to translate the gender wars and especially to invite sympathy for its outmatched males was especially valuable in a world which found itself increasingly lacking the coordinates to map newly reconfigured sets of gender identities. If the sorts of female successes that this chapter has been documenting left American culture fearful that men's needs and desires would no long figure in a world "overrun" by female ambition, the Douglas character type came to represent the multiple ways in which men were perceived to be newly disenfranchised by this new gender order. Such attributions of disadvantage circumscribe Michael Douglas' role as Dan Gallagher, and, in turn, traversed a number of Douglas star vehicles, including subsequent roles in *Basic Instinct* (1992), *Falling Down* (1993), and *Disclosure* (1994), each of which cast Douglas as victimized by systems no longer sympathetic to the rights of the white man. As Linda Ruth Williams writes, "he is often figured as *the* representation of flawed, crisis-ridden masculinity and the concomitant decline of male cultural and social authority" (2005: 177).

Douglas' role in *Basic Instinct*, for instance, cast him as a disgraced cop cowed by his attraction to author Catherine Tramell (Sharon Stone), a femme fatale suspected of murdering men without compunction. Once again positioned between the good girl and bad girl, the unlucky man in this portrayal finds he cannot resist the femme fatale's polymorphous perversity or her kinky sexual proclivities. Yet the film simultaneously reminds audiences, especially in its famous final shot of the icepick under the bed, of the steep price men pay for dallying with such women. A similar ideology animates *Disclosure*, wherein Douglas finds himself the victim of a merciless and ambitious co-worker Meredith (Demi Moore), with whom he formerly had a relationship. She tries to seduce him again and, though he successfully rebuffs her advances, she becomes enraged and retaliatory in the face of his rejection, forcing him to bring charges of sexual harassment against her. The film thereby emphasizes the anxious economies that seem destined to disenfranchise men, all the while observing how castrating women occupy positions of domination. Cynical about the fact that ordinary men enjoy none of patriarchy's supposed privileges, *Disclosure* identifies men as society's main victims, an observation underscored by a running subplot about the threat of layoffs and redundancy. Again, *Disclosure* understands feminist gains through a backlash narrative that believes women to have unfairly usurped male jobs and male power.

The multiple failures of the Douglas persona thread together his film roles; whether single and damaged as in *Basic Instinct*, or as a failed family man in *War of the Roses*, *Fatal Attraction*, *Falling Down*, *Disclosure*, and *Traffic* (2000), his appearances collectively feature him being taken advantage of, stalked, and often outmaneuvered by unscrupulous women. Additionally, because the women are pathological and often deranged, it is not a stretch to say that they elicit justifiably fearful responses – a world at the mercy of powerful women, according to such a paradigm, lacks moral stability. Collectively, such portrayals work in tandem with the feminist backlash for they script feminist gains as inevitably de-feminizing and marshal audience sympathy in favor of male victims whose disenfranchisement is systematized and inevitable.

One can therefore liken Alex Forrest to the other delusional or otherwise misguided working women whom the Douglas character encounters, women who courted resentment from a culture unhappy about their new status or roles.[10] As well, such women began to populate a variety of mass cultural forms, and Close's portrayal in *Fatal Attraction* dialogued with other career woman films (or "new woman" films) that emerged in relatively the same cultural moment. Films as such as *Baby Boom* (1987), *Broadcast News* (1987), *Working Girl* (1988), *The Good Mother* (1988), and *Presumed Innocent* (1990) featured professional women who revisit their career aspirations, most often because they meet a man who teaches them to downshift their career, or because they are punished for having sexual and professional ambitions thought unbefitting to a woman. As Amelia Jones argues, new woman's films exhibit a deep determination to close down the independent woman's professional and sexual independence, and are motivated by male paranoia over the breakdown of traditional rules governing sexual structures. Thus, she believes that these films "work to punish these deviant women or reinscribe them within traditional familial structures" (1991: 297). While Alex's bloody fate makes it clear that she is punished rather than reformed, *Fatal Attraction* stands as a prototype for the tale of female aspirations gone awry and (despite its producers' declarations to the contrary) was hardly a singular idiosyncratic story of one career woman gone crazy.

Instead, Alex rounds out a cast of cinematic women starring in films that pivot around the question of how to resolve the unique problem of career women, females who needed cinematic rehabilitation to rid them of pretenses to economic or cultural gain. Diane Keaton's power hungry J. C. Wiatt in *Baby Boom*, for instance, is schooled on the virtues of maternal generosity, a lesson that arrives via the inheritance of an unexpected child. This upheaval results in her eventual relocation to Vermont, the abandonment of a lucrative corporate career, and a rugged, masculine boyfriend who serves as a replacement for the caricatured yuppies who populate her existence as a Manhattanite. While *Baby Boom* lovingly chides its ambitious female into a posture of supplication through a series of emotional rewards, the fates are typically not so rosy for the women coded as sexually and economically ambitious. Sigourney Weaver, who plays the ruthless, backstabbing boss Katherine Parker in *Working Girl*, gets her "bony ass" handed to her when she loses both her job and her boyfriend to the more compliant Tess McGill (Melanie Griffith), and the film rewards Tess's unthreatening perseverance with a climb up the corporate ladder. *Presumed Innocent* likewise organizes its narrative around the murder investigation of Carolyn Polhemus (Greta Scacchi), a calculating and sexually aggressive prosecutor murdered, we finally learn, by the wife of the man with whom she was having an affair. Carolyn's fate collides rather explicitly with Alex's, and, as Amelia Jones observes, both films "invent the new woman as a caricature of masculinized femininity in order to annihilate her, as if to prove that a woman's ability to be both professionally and sexually empowered is intolerable" (1991: 307). As well, both Carolyn and Alex are murdered by the wives of their male lovers, conventionally feminine women who find they cannot abide by the familial violations the aggressive woman has wrought. Collectively, these backlash narratives suggest that the conundrum of female ambition and success can best be resolved by denying the ambitious woman permission to continue as she is, either because she is forcibly recuperated into traditional patriarchal structures through shame or embarrassment or, conversely, because she is killed.

Though *Fatal Attraction* did not necessarily inaugurate the "rehabilitate or remove" solution to the problem of the unwieldy career woman, it was nonetheless the most popular film to count itself as openly suspicious of such women, and its attempt to both censor and censure Alex proved wildly successful. Offering Alex as a caricature that it invited audiences to hate, the film avoided the messy complexities of the real issues confronting working women, all the while benefitting from a cultural era wherein audiences did not take much convincing to look askance at the career woman. Alex's outright villainy, and her determination to annihilate her romantic rivals easily provides audiences with ample justification for their ill-will against her, thereby efficiently mobilizing cultural anxieties surrounding career women in a guilt free orgy of retributional anger. In this way, audiences get to have it both ways: it is pleasurable to hate Alex, the difficult and undeserving career woman, and especially pleasurable not to have to feel guilty doing so.[11]

It's a Wrap ... Redux

Perhaps the best example of the film's attempts to punish the career woman is to be found in its multiple rewritings of its multiple endings, whereby each successive incarnation waters down the seriousness of Dan's fate and in turn ratchets up the severity of Alex's. *Fatal Attraction*'s crowd-pleaser finale, where Alex dies brutally at the end of a handgun fired by Beth, was in fact the fourth ending written for the film, and represents a concession to test audiences who were adamant in their demand that Alex meet a gruesome fate befitting her crime. *Fatal Attraction*'s process of trial and error bespeaks a parable wherein the ultimate point of the film came to be the preservation of patriarchal power, a sensibility that the initial endings considered for the film did not share.

James Dearden's original script for *Fatal Attraction* was called *Affairs of the Heart*, and Alex Forrest was named Eve Rubin, a nomenclature that evoked both the temptation of the biblical Eve and a Jewish heritage, both of which were radically altered in the rewriting process. In this ending, which was never filmed, Alex kills herself by plunging a nine-inch knife into her abdomen, and succeeds in framing Dan for her murder because his prints are still on the knife. No exculpating evidence arrives to exonerate him, and this version ends in pure nihilism, since, although Dan protests that he has not committed the murder, the hand of justice nevertheless comes down swiftly and harshly. The scene from the original screenplay reads:

DAN: I'm innocent. I swear to God, I am innocent!
INT PRISON CELL NIGHT
DAN stands in the doorway of a small cell. He turns to face the camera.
DAN: I am innocent!
The cell door slams in his face.
CUT TO BLACK (quoted in Williams, 2005: 185)[12]

Because this ending makes Dan "pay" for his crimes, it challenges patriarchal authority in unprecedented ways. It refuses to let Dan get away with using Alex, and instead presents a vision of a world that punishes haphazard mistakes with exacting vengeance. One might argue, of course, that such an ending suggests that male paranoia is justified, since even beyond the grave Alex wreaks havoc. Nevertheless, the ending remains as unbending as Dan's fate, since it suggests that retribution will undermine what was heretofore his easy privilege.

Though this ending was quickly discarded, it was nevertheless inspirational for the finale that was planned and filmed, wherein Dan and his family are accosted by three police officers in his front yard and told that Alex's throat was slit by a knife which contains Dan's fingerprints. The police then haul Dan away. Initially, this was supposed to be the penultimate scene (the final being Alex's suicide) although Lyne subsequently tacked on a slightly more forgiving version of the sequence wherein Dan tells Beth to contact one of his coworkers. In the process of thumbing through Dan's address book in his attic study, Beth finds the tape that Alex has made for her husband. As she is phoning, Beth listens to the tape and hears what is tantamount to a confession from Alex. As Alex says, tonelessly, "I'll just cut deeper next time. I'll kill myself. I will. There's nothing else left for me, Dan. Nothing, nothing." In classic *deus ex machina* fashion, Alex's tape will presumably clear Dan's name.

Dan's exculpation is assumed here, but never actually shown. While Beth leaves the house to free Dan, calling to Ellen in a voiceoff, the film ends with a flashback of Alex's suicide, as she sits on the floor of her white bathroom, and slits her throat to the tune of *Madame Butterfly*. In many ways, this ending ties together the various thematics the film developed – the knife that Dan gripped and left on Alex's

In the film's original ending, Alex committed suicide and framed Dan for her murder.

counter is the same one she uses to frame him, and the tragic swells of *Madame Butterfly* provide the soundtrack for Alex's suicide.[13] Yet, American test audiences were dramatically unsatisfied by this denouement, perhaps because Alex becomes the film's main tragic figure, rather than Dan or the family she has harmed. Screening the film for audiences in Seattle, San Francisco, and Los Angeles, Lyne said that he sensed a feeling of deflation among the test viewers, and Dearden agreed that the ending was "not cathartic." Dearden explains, "They'd grown to hate this woman by this time, to the degree that they actually wanted him [Dan] to have some retribution" (quoted in Faludi, 1991: 122).[14] As well, Williams argues that "what the disappointed preview audience experienced was a kind of cinematic coitus interruptus" (2005: 56). Invoking the sexual act, such conversations likened the experience of film-going to orgasm, such that a good film, like good sex, creates the build-up of anticipation and sees that build-up through to completion. This comparison nevertheless had a decidedly misogynist subtext since, as Joyce Thompson argues, the "choice of words here suggests the need for a sexual as well as emotional release that can best be achieved by an act of violence against the woman whom the audience has been manipulated to hate" (1992: 13). Put in these terms, it is hard not to think of Alex's final defeat as a moment of ejaculation not only for Dan, but also Beth, who in a sense adopts the phallus when she shoots Alex.

The $1.3 million alteration, which was filmed months after the film wrapped, capitulated to a desire for catharsis and retribution as well as served as a dramatic show of force that will presumably help to rebuild the fractured family unit. However, while popular, this ending was widely thought to reduce the film's overall artistic value. For many the final bathroom sequence confirmed that the film degenerated into a predictable thriller, and *Fatal Attraction*'s producers, stars, and director all expressed ambivalence over the question of whether the reshot ending was actually faithful to the rest of the film.[15] Surprisingly, despite the fact that that they were ones who decided on the alternate ending, director Lyne and producers Stanley Jaffe and Sherry Lansing credit audience reaction as their motivating impulse. The now-codified explanation for the film's alteration turns on the creators' supposed shock that audiences had so much anger toward Alex, anger that the producers felt they in turn had to accommodate. Lyne has said of Alex, "my sympathies were with her for longer than the audience's. I saw her as a tragic and lonely figure" (Hirschberg, 1987: 14). Regardless of the industry politics that went into this decision, the explanation that audiences were behind the demand for a different resolution is significant, for it shows how the film became memorialized as having responded to, rather than having created and inflamed, the battle over feminine identities. Supposedly answering a cultural need rather than creating one, *Fatal Attraction* is often taken as evidencing a deep, barely concealed desire on the part of American audiences to see the nuclear family unit triumph over the dislocations enforced by the single career woman. This convenient position deftly sidesteps the film's many methods of inflaming and pandering to these problematic desires, and omits the role it continues to play in rendering gender battles in the most divisive terms possible.

As well, the new ending confirmed that this was a battle to be fought *between* women, for it complies with a perceived demand for a confrontation between the sparring women, granting Alex a spectacular death that in turn excludes the impotent man. Indeed, the film had been tending in this direction since Beth tells Alex that if she ever comes near her family again, she will kill Alex. Faithful to this threat, the new ending fronts the issue of female rage and revenge, and in turn acknowledges that the competition between Beth and Alex stands as the film's foremost duel. Chapter Five examines how this straw battle serves as a parable for the feminist movement in a postfeminist age, which reframes feminist issues as conflicts between women. The film's status as a sort of wish fulfillment whereby the career woman bears the brunt of cultural anxiety and suffers as a result thereby heralded an important moment in the on-going gender wars, since it confirmed through bloody triumph the preeminence of women whose lives are culturally sanctioned.

Chapter 4

Erotic Sexuality, AIDS, and the Case for Staying Faithful

Widely understood as the film that would "terrify men into being faithful," *Fatal Attraction*'s tale of a man haunted by an unplanned sexual encounter took particular aim at the erotically adventurous. As reviewer Fred Bruning put it, *Fatal Attraction* is "perhaps the most effective deterrent to illicit sex since stoning" (1987: 7). Such attributions fueled rather than stalled the viewing frenzy surrounding the film in its opening weeks, as stories abounded about how wives dragged their husbands to the film in droves, bent on shriveling libidos in a ritual of public shaming that amounted to a two-hour harangue against the risks of infidelity. Corroborated by public testimonials, reviewers described the spectacle occurring outside the *Fatal Attraction* theater: couples emerging out of the darkness looking sideways at one another, girlfriends telling boyfriends that they would not hesitate to castrate him if he ever tried such a stunt, and shell-shocked men accosting director Adrian Lyne with a sarcastic "thanks a lot."[1] At the same time, real life *Fatal Attraction* stories captivated the nation; roughly a month after the film's release, *People Weekly* featured a story about women and men driven to stalking and stabbings, all testaments to the dangers of amorous liaisons gone bad. Oprah Winfrey and Phil Donahue subsequently interviewed real-life *Fatal Attraction* candidates, using their respective shows as vehicles to engage public debate on the prevalence of infidelity in contemporary culture. These iterations of the disastrous consequences of impulse attraction generally lacked both substance and subtlety, yet for everyone who saw or even heard about *Fatal Attraction*, one takeaway message from this collective viewing event was abundantly clear: sex has consequences.

The discourse surrounding *Fatal Attraction*'s ascendance quickly took on the character of a moral panic in 1987, one whose logic nevertheless followed a sort of Foucauldian model. While audiences reveled in the graphic sexuality of the film and its various perversions, they were at the same time lashed for exhibiting the prurience that was in fact the film's bread and butter appeal. A cultural coitus interruptus if you will, *Fatal Attraction* both invited desires and then swiftly punished those who demonstrated them, taking audiences from a moment of heightened sexual desire to a swift and violent rebuke. By soliciting desires to show their danger, the film thereby made masochism a mode of its appeal, handholding audiences through the pleasure of pain. As this chapter explores, such a cinematic ethos marked a definitive end to the sexual revolution thanks to its coupling of erotic sexuality with debilitating consequence. Elliptically linking casual sex to illegitimate pregnancy, disease, and AIDS, the film was not subtle about its investment in a stark cause-and-effect logic that yoked sexual indiscretion to catastrophe; as *Rolling Stone* reviewer Lisa Henricksson wrote: "Fuck-and-die movies, a friend calls them, and the biggest F & D of them all was *Fatal Attraction*" (1987: 147).

While the sexual caution was clearly linked to the effect of unplanned sex on the body, the film's obsession with the deadly consequences of sex also had a clear socioeconomic subtext. *Fatal Attraction*'s extreme scare tactics were put in service of protecting the middle-class family – the repository of the national imaginary in the Reagan era – from the contaminants unleashed by sexual perversions. In the socio-historical terms set forth by the film, infidelity exists as a scourge that threatens not only Dan Gallagher, but also imperils his health, his home, his profession, his class status, and his path to upward mobility.

Sexual Caution: Proceed at Your Own Risk

Fatal Attraction peppers its narrative with recognitions of the dangers of sex, attributions inaugurated the first time Dan and Beth leave their house together. At a book launch fete, Dan and Beth encounter Dan's boss, who, Dan says, injured himself while coupling with his wife. This sentiment emerges in the film's first public scene, unmistakably correlating the act of Dan's and Beth's departure from the comfortable space of their house to sex's unforeseen consequences. Dan's boss sports a wide neck brace and Dan jokes to Beth, "You should see his wife." At a business meeting the next morning, the perils of sex again arise conversationally – the Saturday-morning powwow has been necessitated by a potentially explosive fiction written by a female author Alex represents, and the author has been accused of basing her narrative on a real-life affair with a married senator now threatening to sue. Though the manuscript represents a palimpsest of the author's experiences, Alex impishly admits that it is in part a *roman-à-clef* about this particular man, for the author did have an affair with the senator. In this, the scene foreshadows Dan's eventual likeness to the disgraced senator, as he too will try to quell the tide which threatens his reputation and well-being.[2]

While these two events frame sex as accidentally or inadvertently dangerous, when Dan and Alex partake of their amorous encounter the very nature of their sex appears perilous. Alex leads Dan into the meatpacking district, a modern-day Hades, where her apartment resides, and the mise en scène imbues the sexual encounter with a sinister effect. During the encounter, Alex perches uncomfortably on top of a sink. Later, the couple risks exposure when Alex performs fellatio on Dan in the open-air elevator, sexual contortions which link pleasure, exhibitionism, and peril. The film thus repeatedly maps a sexual relationship that shares its coordinates with pain infliction, as evidenced by Dan's panting exhaustion after their first lovemaking session, his grimacing face during the elevator fellatio, and Alex's physical attack on him shortly after their tryst, when she begins beating his chest and rips his shirt. Noticing the extent to which physical harm circumscribes this relationship, Mandy Merck argues that the film's presentation of sexuality imitates the primal scene, wherein, "an act of coition is equated with violence and silently witnessed by a third party" (1988: 98). According to the Freudian paradigm, the primal scene traumatizes the child who inadvertently witnesses the

Dan bumbles his way to the bed, with his pants around his ankles.

sexual encounter between his parents, believes his father to be killing rather than making love to his mother, and perceives sex as a violent violation. *Fatal Attraction* maps sexuality in somewhat similar terms, putting audiences in the position of the witnessing child who stands a party to the violence of the sexual encounter.[3] In their first sexual encounters, however, it might appear that Alex is the one "killing" Dan, since his response is the one largely indistinguishable as pleasure or pain.

The establishment of the sex/pleasure/pain equation repeats itself in the attack scenes, which make unconscious alignment between impulses of violence and those of desire. The male takes up his rightful position as the aggressor, however, since Dan attempts to kill Alex, thereby literalizing the fear that animates the trauma experienced by the spectator to the primal scene. In this way, spectators are in the position of the watching child who nonetheless finds his fears confirmed; because Dan's and Alex's relationship does tend to actual violence, spectators come to understand that sex *can* actually mean death. As described in Chapter One, Dan's attacks on Alex mimic the sexual act, since both parties pant in physical exhaustion as Dan attempts to strangle her, and she lunges at him with a knife. Sex and violence appear then not only as interrelated drives, rather, the attack sequence doubles back to the sex scene, thereby elucidating that sex is pleasurable because it *is* dangerous.[4]

The film, however, does not languish for long in these pleasurable perversions. In what David Andrews calls a "frontloaded" organizational structure, the sex itself takes up a relatively short amount of narrative space, leaving ample time for a detailed investigation of its

Passion turns quickly to danger; here, Alex attacks Dan with a butcher knife.

fallout (2006: 64).[5] *Fatal Attraction* thereby employs something of a bait and switch approach, indulging the salacious impulses of its characters and its audiences in perhaps the most graphic manner possible, only to turn around and chastise them for having enjoyed the lascivious spectacle that the film willingly offered up. With the exception of the boiled bunny sequence, *Fatal Attraction*'s most recognizable and pleasurable moments are its sex scenes, which are both daring and somewhat shockingly explicit. That such graphic depictions were allowed to flourish *sans* an X rating bespeaks at least some degree of cultural permissiveness, one that benefited from loosening standards of sexual propriety and, in turn, willingness on the part of filmmakers and distributors to market films with graphic content. During the sexual revolution of the 1960s and 1970s, more liberal standards of sexual behavior were both encouraged by, and reflected in, media representations. *Fatal Attraction* owes a debt to this era, wherein sexual portrayals were not bound, as the previous code regulations mandated, to euphemize illicit sexuality. Yet, while *Fatal Attraction* clearly utilizes these expanded representational prerogatives to its own ends, it does so guiltily, making its characters and audiences pay for the erotic encounters they have so enjoyed.

The uneasiness that characterizes this position is evidenced by the efficiency of the punishing hand of justice, and marked by the rapid turnabout in the film's emotional tenor. Desire quickly gives way to fear, a shift underscored by the fact that the film refuses to allow Dan even the briefest opportunity to bask in a post-coital glow. Instead, Alex attacks him immediately after their final lovemaking session, chastising him with the observation that she is not happy about the fact that he rushes out after "every time we make love." Notably, Dan has *literally* just exited the bed when the harangue begins; to punctuate this point, Alex attempts suicide only minutes later. The proximity of the sex to the verbal lashing and the later self-immolation bespeaks a narrative break, a shift from indulgence to retribution, as the film will heretofore abandon its devil-may-care attitude, its humor, and its jocular sensibility. (Even subsequent scenes wherein Dan seems light-hearted, such as when he entertains guests in his home, are pierced through by reminders of his affair's consequence.) The rapidity of the turnabout and the permanence of the devastation that follows align the pacing of the film with Dan's emotional trajectory, wherein the movement from passion to pain will heretofore be uni-directional.

As well, the film manifests the effects of his affair on Dan's family dynamic, which it speaks through multiple lingering shots of Dan looking longingly at his wife and daughter. These shots throb with unspoken remorse, for the affair robs Dan of the ability to fully communicate with his loved ones, since he cannot tell them what he has done. The confession scene, which follows on the heels of the boiled bunny sequence, additionally marks the moment wherein the effects of Dan's indiscretions migrate from his tortured psychology to the bodies of his wife and child. Ellen lies tearful in bed mourning the loss of Whitey, and Beth gets increasingly hysterical as Dan reveals his affair. Unbeknownst to Dan or Beth, however, Ellen witnesses the escalating argument, tearfully watching from a doorway as her mother screams at Dan, "What is the matter with you?!" after he admits not only that he has had an affair, but that Alex is pregnant.[6] The sequences surrounding Dan's confession and subsequent expulsion from the family home draw acute attention to Ellen's suffering as an embodied emotion. Both the scene where he leaves, looking in on his sleeping daughter, and the scenes where Dan calls her from a stark hotel room act as rejoinders to Dan, as Ellen asks Dan if he will call tomorrow, and Dan's tone indicates wistful deflation. The brutal toll the affair takes is echoed shortly thereafter in Beth's accident and literalized by her black eye and bruised body. Martyred, the two females clearly suffer for Dan's sins.

While the collateral damage of Dan's extramarital escapades includes the victimization of his innocent wife and daughter, the film also punishes its not-so-innocent spectators, those who have presumably enjoyed the sexual spectacle in all its hedonistic indulgence. In this way, the film solicits the same set of emotional outcomes from the audience as it does from Dan – both begin the film in titillation, and end in terror. Michael Douglas described precisely such a trajectory when he offered his estimation of how audiences responded to the film: "People leave saying 'I laughed, I got turned on by the sex scenes, and I got scared'" (Corliss, 1987: 73). The film thereby marches spectators through a trajectory that proceeds blatantly from pleasure to pain: using spectators' desire to see and know against them, the film devises a "punishment befitting the crime" in that, while it happily allows audiences the voyeuristic pleasure of witnessing the sexual encounter, it later implicates us as perpetrators in Alex's reign of terror. Such implication can be found, for instance, when the camera accompanies Alex as she surreptitiously follows Dan home, or when, after Beth realizes her daughter is missing, audiences see Alex and Ellen strolling through the amusement park. In each, the audience's point of view departs from Dan's, thereby burdening us with unwanted knowledge and serving as symbolic chastisement for our previously pleasurable voyeurism. While the enjoyment of viewership stems in part from the ability to watch illicit activities from a position of comfortable secrecy, such a position is immobilizing since with anonymity also comes impotence. Just as Dan has no recourse for neutralizing Alex, audiences are painfully reminded of our inability to warn the family of Alex's encroachment, or to soothe Dan and Beth with the knowledge that, despite Ellen's absence from school, she is not being harmed. Such sequences produce a sort of immersion therapy whereby they associate scopophilic impulses with suffering rather than seduction.[7]

Both swift and fleeting, sexual enjoyment in *Fatal Attraction* is instrumentalized as an object lesson – no sooner do those who partake in sexual escapades, as well as those who either mistakenly or pleasurably witness them, find their libidos tickled than they come to see the danger of such a position. Remorse visits directly on the heels of sexual titillation, a congruence that provides insight into why the film so successfully served a prophylactic function in terms of its presentation of extramarital sexuality. Because the film is paced in accordance with Dan's psychic register, it efficaciously transforms itself into a cautionary tale as both Dan and audiences come to regret their seduction by the sexual spectacle.

Hangovers of the Sexual Revolution: Birth Control, Pregnancy, and AIDS

Fatal Attraction revels in but then disavows its eroticism; despite acknowledging the short-term pleasures heralded by sexual freedom, in the long run, it argues, extramarital sex is simply not worth it. (As discussed in Chapter Three, a similar observation regarding the paradoxical limitations occasioned by freedom energizes the film's presentation of the feminist revolution. Though women may credit feminist gain with newfound independence, the film forecasts for them a dim future, bereft of husbands or children.) A clear beneficiary of the sexual revolution, *Fatal Attraction* begins by stressing how relaxations in sexual codes circumscribe Dan's affair – namely, he finds in Alex a willing and inventive sexual partner, one without moral hang-ups surrounding the act of extramarital sex. Alex titillates thanks to her refusal to be bound by conventional notions of sexual propriety, and the affair is made possible (and pleasurable) thanks to her unapologetic sexual appetites. Alex's sexual liberation therefore allows Dan to indulge prurient impulses and grants him the pleasure of indulging in sexual behaviors unregulated by standards of decorum or overlaid with the representative pressures of "marital sex."

That pleasure, though, proves fleeting, an eventuality the film partly traces to the fact that the parameters for how the affair should proceed in the wake of the sex lack definition. In this way, *Fatal Attraction* maps out a dynamic that is central to the postsexual revolutionary period and in turn to a postfeminist age, since it suggests that the gains to be gotten from a widespread relaxation of sexual mores have nevertheless occasioned a widespread cultural implosion. Specifically, while sexual license can be taken by everyone, the order lacks a corresponding set of guiding principles for negotiating the ensuing gender politics that such relaxations occasion. Though the sexes may think they can "read" one another, in fact, the semiotic parameters of this process continually shift. While Alex might be apprehended, for instance, as a female with a free-flying libido, a liberated woman in touch with her sexuality, this estimation is rendered quickly illegitimate when Alex's sexual appetites are unmasked as a posture merely to seduce Dan into a more significant commitment. Alex promises a "no-strings-attached" relationship, a negotiation that takes places over a dinnertime conversation wherein Alex asks Dan if he is "discreet," their suggestive bantering an invitation for the raucous sex that follows. Yet, despite Alex's assurance that she too can be counted on to act responsibly ("We're two adults" she says) she delivers completely the opposite, since she soon demands a permanent position in Dan's life. This bait and switch gives the lie to discourses of female sexuality which claim that sexual pleasure can be an end in itself, since audiences come to understand that Alex fibbed when she promised that she could have sex without emotional or physical consequence. Indeed, she forces both – she claims to be in love with Dan, and she foists an unwanted pregnancy on him. In this way, Alex reveals the film's belief that, though women may claim sexual freedom, and purport to desire a sexual relationship free of commitment or intimacy, they nevertheless hold the perverse power to redefine the meaning of those terms. Even worse, it suggests that Alex holds the man responsible when she effects such a redefinition, though it implicitly asks, how was he to know that she would do so?

This paradigm unmasks the film's belief that sexual liberation ushers in a period where citizens are left adrift in a sea of discursive uncertainty, a reality that also organizes the film's treatment of birth control. Dan assumes Alex uses some form of contraception, a belief stemming from his (apparently naïve) willingness to trust Alex when she says she want sex for itself – to him, this also means that she will take precautions not to become pregnant. The way this is supposed to work, the film reminds us, is for men to be able to enjoy the benefit of sex without having to indulge nagging suspicions that women are using the act to entrap them. Yet, the postfeminist logic that animates *Fatal Attraction* suggests otherwise, for the specter of Alex's unplanned pregnancy confirms that, while men can perhaps take unprecedented sexual license, they nevertheless still need to trust women to accurately represent their sexual and reproductive inclinations. The danger of abandoning conventional ideals of sexual chastity seems to be that women present their sexual predilections in one way and dramatically revise those intentions and their outcomes once the man's back is figuratively turned. In such a climate of mistrust, it would apparently be prudent of men not to believe what women *say* they want.

If the sexual revolution was made possible in part by the wide availability and reliability of various forms of birth control, *Fatal Attraction*'s pregnancy subplot forces the recognition that birth control does not happen by itself, and that one needs to trust (perhaps untrustworthy) women to practice it. Alex's marauding sexuality has various ulterior motives, since she apparently was not practicing birth control during their affair – a fact that Dan thinks to ask her about only *after* she announces her pregnancy. As Alex admits, she had a miscarriage in the past, and did not believe she could get pregnant again. *Sans* women who will reliably participate in family planning, sexual freedom clearly loses some of its appeal; in turn, the film wistfully longs for bygone eras wherein men assumed women *did* want children, and were thereby cognizant of the risks they took in engaging in a sexual liaison. Dan solicits sympathy because he did not know what he was getting himself into, a defense of ignorance rendered plausible because it suggests that, while women may say they want sexual freedom, they are nonetheless willing to lie about it, thus forcing the conclusion that men cannot be held accountable for believing them.

Viewing sexual liberation as an organizational model that ultimately disenfranchises men – an attitude uncomfortably akin to its position on feminism – the film sets up a formulation whereby Dan emerges as the primary victim of unfettered sexual exploration. As Angela McRobbie observes, "*Fatal Attraction* brings into being a cultural sensibility which allows men to feel they have been wronged by women, or that they might find themselves wronged by women. From now on they must be on their guard, they must defend themselves against a kind of violent sexual exploitation by women" (2008: 40). The primary marker of such "exploitation" is of course Alex's unplanned pregnancy, since Dan is unwittingly burdened with a responsibility he had no intention of inviting. Taking this fact into account, feminist Karen Durbin claims that it is Dan who *metaphorically* gets impregnated, since he recalls the classic female nightmare of that "huge distressing, apparently endless consequence he cannot rid himself of" (1987: 90). As Durbin also notes, it is Dan rather than Alex who wants and desires the abortion, but is told that this is not his decision to make. Perhaps recalling the longstanding governmental prohibitions on this practice, made mostly at the discretion of male doctors and legislators who decided women's reproductive fates, Durbin writes, "O role reversal! O bitter joy!" (1987: 90).

While Durbin gleefully revels in the resonance between Dan's position and the historical lot of women who needed abortions and were told they could not procure them, her viewpoint nonetheless stands in opposition to a more widespread sense that there is real pathos in Dan's position. While Durbin may take pleasure in the seeming intractability of Dan's situation, the film nonetheless encourages the viewpoint that, if Alex would simply agree to an abortion, Dan could still successfully extract himself from this situation and return to his "normal" life. Stunned at the lack of power he has with respect to her pregnancy, Dan asks Alex, "I don't have a say in this?" as he stands flanked by a large billboard that mocks him with a picture of newlyweds on a boat toasting their good fortune with the words "a glorious beginning." The hopeful image frames and ironizes his situation, as Dan pauses in a crowded, dirty subway, with the dawning consciousness that he has impregnated a woman he is slowly starting to hate. Though Dan's investment in terminating the pregnancy matches the ferocious desire with which Alex wants to see it through, this scene underscores that she alone holds the power to make this decision. The film therefore reads abortion in much the same way that it reads birth control, as a practice over which women have unfair or perhaps undue influence.

Placed in the vice grip of Alex's determination to carry the pregnancy to term, the film thus inadvertently (and perhaps unintentionally) advocates a pro-choice stand. Yet, such a stand is, as the ironic visuals of this scene attest, the result of a series of moral gymnastics premised most heavily on protecting the sacrosanct nuclear family, a unit whose whiteness further underscores the legitimacy of their claim to propagate without disturbance. The film advocates abortion for Alex not because it believes in women's choice, but rather because abortion remains one of the few options left by which to preserve the patriarchal priorities of the upper-middle-class family, and to defend it against the incursions of an unwanted intruder. In this, the film backhandedly justifies abortion through a conservative family values logic; the unborn fetus is not the innocent baby praised in pro-life rhetoric, but rather a disruption to patriarchal prerogative and worthy of termination on this score.[8] That abortion can be supported from a right-leaning perspective is nevertheless telling, for Reagan era America was already rumbling with anti-abortion sentiment, and Reagan's Supreme Court nominee Robert Bork was vetted the same year, a confirmation hearing that turned largely on his pro-life views. While *Fatal Attraction* would seem to fall squarely into a conservative camp which lamented abortion's legalization, the film nevertheless advocates for it, although it does so from a position that borders nervously on eugenics. Actively advocating a hierarchal structure whereby only some families are worth protecting, *Fatal Attraction* naturalizes the idea that Dan's white nuclear family does not merit disruption. Like the marginalized "welfare mothers" whose out-of-wedlock births were excoriated as shameful and irresponsible in 1980s political culture, Alex's pregnancy is too coded as an unnecessary indulgence, a signal of her moral depravity. In much the same way that unmarried women, often women of color, were told that they had no right to have children without a "proper" family structure in place, the film encourages the estimation that Alex's pregnancy is wasteful and self-serving, and has no problem dispensing with it when the time is right.

Fatal Attraction needs the eradication of this pregnancy to maintain the boundaries between the Gallagher family and its negative inverse. Short of forcing Alex into the abortion clinic at gunpoint, however,

Dan cannot bring the procedure about, and thus the film resorts to a narrative rather than clinical solution to the problem of Alex's pregnancy. Notably, both the film's original ending and the one that was reshot postproduction result in the pregnancy's early termination; whether she is killed by Beth, or whether she commits suicide, both endings ensure that Dan's and Alex's baby will never be born. This outcome is so desirable – and indeed, so necessary – to the story *Fatal Attraction* wants to tell that, when Beth kills Alex at the film's conclusion, no acknowledgement is made of the fact that two lives have been taken. That this reality is neither acknowledged nor mourned suggests the ways in which the film instrumentalizes this pregnancy as a hindrance to Dan, seeing it only as more trace evidence of Alex's selfishness and refusal to bend to his will.[9]

While *Fatal Attraction* centralizes a dialogue about the reproductive consequences of sexuality, it was also thought to participate in a shadow conversation about the burgeoning AIDS crisis in the United States. Describing how the disease circulated in cultural products even when not made explicit, Foster Hirsch writes, "Erotic thrillers of the 1980s and 1990s are metaphors for the dangers of sex in a time of AIDS. A simmering offstage 'noise' like World War II in 1940s noir, AIDS is a significant structuring absence" (quoted in Williams, 2005: 30). A devastating disease that was both transmitted through sexual contact and tainted with attributions of immorality because it was stereotypically associated with supposedly "deviant" sexual practices such as homosexuality and/or having multiple sexual partners, AIDS served as a metaphor for the retribution visited upon illicit sexuality. Framing sexual practices as matters of morality and consequence, *Fatal Attraction* clearly borrows from this organizational model in that it too sees Dan's "immoral" sexual activities as having been the catalyst for his imperiled state. Because he defied the tenets of marriage and monogamy in favor of casual sex, it argues, he brought this scourge upon himself.

According to the film's logic, anything but the most normative and sanctioned sexual practices will result in deadly consequence, especially any type of casual, unplanned, or unprotected sex. This perceived corollary between sex and danger can also be explained by the fact that both Dan's predicament and the one experienced by those who contract AIDS from sexual contact similarly engage in pleasurable behaviors, behaviors whose severe risks are only later revealed. The attribution of the film as an AIDS parable acknow-ledges this newfound cultural alignment between risk and sexual contact and the disease was widely touted as putting an end to an era of "casual sex" precisely because the consequences of behaviors that were once seen as harmless were not only dangerous, but often deadly. In addition, the rapidity of the act in contrast to the permanence of the affliction resonates with Alex's plan to keep the child; as Dan says in a desperate plea to get Alex to reconsider her decision, "Just think about this, we are gonna live with this for the rest of our lives."

The syllogism between adultery and AIDS also positions Alex *as* the disease – Linda Ruth Williams writes that "in that *Fatal Attraction* was cast as an AIDS parable about the consequences of casual sex, it casts Alex as the contagious agent – both the channel of the contagion and the location of the symptom" (2005: 54). In such a formulation, Alex is, first, the carrier of the AIDS virus. Sleeping with her is the action that infects Dan, thus she should be considered the one in whom the disease manifests itself. Yet, once transmitted to Dan, the disease does not merely take up residence in him, since the disease he acquires, the virus of which he cannot rid himself, is *also* her. Alex is thus the carrier and the symptom, and Dan can neither escape what she has done to him nor escape her. Like a recurring affliction, Alex keeps returning unexpectedly and inopportunely, every appearance confirming her now permanent position in Dan's life.

As well, Dan appears as a "carrier" in his own right, since having the disease alienates him from his own family, separating him from their safe, healthy, undisturbed realm. At the same time, he must protect his family by hiding them from Alex, thereby shielding them from the contamination. As Judith Williamson writes, "if the underlying threat is infection, Dan's fear must simply be Alex/the virus reaching his wife and child" (1993: 67). This identification of Alex as an infectious pathogen speaks as well to the film's interest in policing the borders of the family home, a trope that was detailed explicitly in Chapter One. Every entry Alex tries to facilitate, whether by phone or in person, is looked upon by Dan with increasing disgust, a reaction that is circumscribed by his estimation of Alex as a contaminating agent. The film thereby links adulterous sexuality – a situation where bodies go into unsanctioned spaces – with the sorts of violations that lead to incurable illness, for they break down the body's defenses. As a syllogism for adultery, AIDS provides an apt comparison because the body wracked by AIDS is one that can no longer protect itself against pathological invasion, and this state of weakened immunity mirrors the status of the Gallagher home, since it too is newly vulnerable to unwanted intrusion. That Alex penetrates the Gallagher home in the final act is highly apt in terms of this metaphor, for it suggests that Dan's unlawful actions have enfeebled what was a previously healthy body. Instead, ripped apart by emotional turmoil, accident, mistrust, violence and disappointment, the familial structure initially lacks the defenses to block the unwanted intruder. That Beth and not Dan is the one to finally immobilize Alex borrows logic from this formulation as well; to provide an antidote to Alex's infection, Beth must be a pure body, which her husband is not.

Adultery and Upward Mobility

Infidelity in *Fatal Attraction* attacks the family from without and implodes the family from within, yet the spatial logics of the affair also proceed laterally, as its effects bleed over into all aspects of Dan's life. Because of the affair, Dan unwittingly participates in an unholy trinity of "immoral" actions – he sires a child out of wedlock, advocates abortion, and faces a divorce from his wife. Dan's infidelity thereby puts him in contact with, and demands his participation in, a host of situations that imperil his status as a morally upstanding individual, participations which in turn imbue his previously unblemished image with the taint of the criminal. Thanks to his adultery, Dan swiftly goes from poster child for the moral majority, the good, law-abiding family man, to its opposite, the potential divorcee with illegitimate children who lies to the police and resorts to violence and murder.

The fact that the film paints Dan's downfall in such tragic terms – indeed, the film is almost biblical in its determination to exact swift retribution – confirms its larger investment in protecting what it sees as rightful familial organizations, as indicated by its stance on abortion. Such organizations turn as well on the alliance between family, work, and notions of the American dream since Dan begins the film as an upwardly mobile capitalist who pledges allegiance to family and his labor, whose life seems to be proceeding according to the preferred script for the young urban professional. He is about to be made partner, and he and Beth are contemplating a move to the suburbs wherein they will embark on home ownership.

These plans are thrown into disarray, however, as a result of Dan's adultery, a disruption that speaks acutely to the ways that adultery tampers with the principles of practical ownership on which socioeconomic rise is predicated. Marriage and private property share an investment in the notion that people can lay claim over other people, and over those things designated as being available for purchase. Though marriage is usually mystified in popular parlance as a relationship of love rather than ownership, the marital pact nevertheless legitimates the act of policing the movements and behaviors of another person. Spouses may not own one another, but they do have a right to surveillance, to dictate where each other's bodies can and cannot go. Adultery interrupts this system of claims in that the wrong people are granted access to the bodies over which they have no "right," an intervention that speaks to the fact that Dan's adultery also imperils his participation in a capitalistic system premised on notions of private ownership. This alliance is formed by the observation that Alex's repeatedly renewed presence in Dan's life risks not only his family stability, but also his path to occupational success, since Alex physically intervenes in his career trajectory when she shows up in his office and makes a nuisance of herself by repeatedly calling him there. Both behaviors reflect Alex's belief that she has a claim on Dan, thereby signaling Dan's failure to preserve his body for its rightful "owner," his wife. When Dan takes Alex through his office, the puzzled stares of his administrative assistant and his best friend speak to the recognition that a foreign being has been introduced in the space, an interloper whose presence signals Dan's inability to stake off his office or his body from cooptation.

The threat that Alex's claim on Dan will pose to his upwardly mobile ambitions is likewise highlighted when Dan and his boss plan a lunch during which they will presumably discuss Dan's application for partner. In the midst of finding a date on the calendar for this lunch, Dan is interrupted by his administrative assistant, who tells him that Alex Forrest is calling again. Alex's interference points out the extent to which the personal interruption bifurcates the professional promise; her presence spears through the conversation, a sharp reminder of the hypocrisy of Dan's image as a "family man." Likewise, immediately preceding this interruption Dan and his boss banter about the house the Gallaghers are buying in the suburbs, a conversation that confirms the extent to which heteronormativity is actively solicited and rewarded in the occupational sector. The moment of corporate approval happens over the specter of the home purchase, yet another sign of how his multiple commitments to ownership culture aid Dan's professional viability. His consideration for partner is clearly connected to his status as a prospective suburbanite, yet adultery imperils both identities since the attribution of Dan as a one-woman family man lacks authenticity. In short, Alex detours Dan's path up the corporate ladder because she has the potential to expose as erroneous the multiple identities he needs for professional success. In this way, the film complies with Barry Keith Grant's notion of the "yuppie horror film," a genre he identified as speaking to the anxieties of an affluent culture in a time of recession. As he argues, because of the valorization of conspicuous wealth in a yuppie worldview, it is less "life" than "lifestyle" that is threatened by the monster, and this observation aptly describes the deleterious effect Alex has on Dan's professional prospects (2004: 166).

The film makes a similar point when Alex's phone calls interrupt Beth's and Dan's dinner party, wherein Dan jokes with his best friends about the impending promotion. Dan ribs his friends with the observation that, once he achieves partnership and moves into the suburbs, they cannot expect to see him every weekend. Yet, the piercing interruption of Alex's call suggests that the affair jeopardizes the same correlation between class and privacy that Dan's conversation attempts to impose. The move up the corporate ladder entails an increasingly privatized existence – bigger houses, bigger cars, and more space, literally, between yourself and your neighbor. Adultery disrupts this spatial expansion, however, because Dan seems to have forfeited precisely this right of privacy as a result of his affair. Specifically, he gives up his ability to maintain a separate home, a place where he can control the space which is, indeed, the implicit promise of ownership.

Dan's inability to bracket off either his living or his work spaces as privately owned also ironically highlights a deficiency in the very area in which he is supposedly an expert. Dan is a *copyright* attorney, a system that ensures people keep what they create, so that one's property, however idiosyncratically defined, cannot be stolen. While Dan earns his livelihood from such knowledge – one of the few substantive work conversations he engages in features him arguing that a case of plagiarism cannot be proven – his personal peccadilloes nevertheless render his family open to similar types of theft. What Alex wants to do, in fact, is to claim Dan's family as hers, in a sense appropriating the Gallagher family script as her own. This act of familial plagiarism is made possible, however, by Dan's adulterous behaviors since they open his family to penetration and disrupt the copyright principle. Dan's sexual behaviors suggest that neither his body nor his family were copyrighted, and thus what he and Beth have – namely, their love, their possessions, and even their daughter – *can* be taken and unlawfully reproduced, just as the plagiarist takes another's idea and calls it her own. As well, Alex's pregnancy can be read as such an attempt at plagiarism, for she wants to physically and literally remake the family Dan already has, reproducing the Gallagher family as an inverted negative in which she occupies the role of wife and mother.[10]

Alex's copyright infringements point out Dan's failures to patent his family, and because she illustrates his deficiency in the arena in which he earns his living, she imperils his status as an upwardly mobile capitalist. At the same time, the film illustrates that capitalistic identities must be preserved at all cost, encouraging the conviction that individuals must take individual action, no matter how violent, to preserve and protect their "rightful" property. In a broader sense, the film invests in neoliberalism, a geopolitical paradigm which encourages citizens to effect "personal responsibility," in effect a code for the fact that the protections and supports once assumed by the government move into the private sector, and into the realm of the family. *Fatal Attraction* complies with a neoliberal worldview in its belief that the individual is entitled to and deserving of private owner-ship, as well as in its conviction that the individual must protect his private property rather than leave such a task up to the distrusted "welfare state." As Janet Karsten Larson explains, in the vision of Lyne's film:

> The found rational premise of behavior is the Yuppie fantasy of the private individual, who lives with his "nuclear family" in an "apartment" and claims the right to murder in defense of his "private property." The film's overt moral about the unprofitableness of a man's vices is as privatistic as its sketched etiology of Alex's neurosis: in this social order aberrant acts and sufferings, in their causes and consequences, are understood, recom-pensed or revenged in wholly individualistic ways. (1988: 79)

The notion that adultery can lead to individual gain or loss structures the film's understanding of why Dan's extramarital acts are erroneous, and also informs the solutions it imagines for righting them. *Fatal Attraction* supports a notion of upward mobility premised on a do-it-yourself model, whereby not only will working hard get you the coveted brass ring – namely, a picturesque home in the suburbs, far from sleazy urban decay – but you will be responsible for stamping out the competition which lies in the way. That such an ethos informs the film explains its investment in spending time with the Gallaghers as they begin to attempt to inhabit and remodel their new house – everyone, including Beth's parents, chips in during the move-in process, unpacking, moving furniture, and painting the new abode. The film's focus on the family as the locus of agency also, however, evinces suspicion in any exogenous group.

This suspicion is most notable in the film's presentation of the police, since the cop to whom Dan appeals for protection appears both bemused by Dan's situation and befuddled about what to do about it. This failing institutional infrastructure lacks the inclination or apparent means to curtail Alex's domestic terrorization, thus the task of subduing her falls to the family itself, prompting reviewers to claim that "the family who kills together, stays together." While this motto is glib, it nonetheless accurately emphasizes the film's investment in extracting the family from any sort of social responsibility or social dependency. According to this logic, no institution or agency will come to Dan's rescue, regardless of the criminality of Alex's behaviors. The neoliberal world evidences distrust of institutionalized organizations and puts the power granted to such organizations back in the hands of the individual, arming them with the potential (and literally the guns) to protect themselves. Alex's defeat at the end of the film can therefore be read as a triumph of the neoliberal ethos in the face of polluting adultery. While adultery contaminates, blurring bodies and domestic spaces, the principle of personal agency and familial loyalty serves as its counterpoint, reaffirming a resolutely privatized world order where people stay in their homes, protect those homes, and do not venture out to help themselves or others.

In this, *Fatal Attraction* is a deeply cynical film, as it confirms a number of prevailing sentiments that have come to organize public life in its historical period and beyond. The film doubts the power of public assistance to come to one's rescue, leaving that protection to the purview of the family itself. It doubts the chance encounter or the accidental meeting, positing these only as dangerous opportunities for vice. It emphasizes sexuality as life-taking rather than life-affirming, as a force best repressed lest it lead to unwanted children or unwanted diseases. It doubts the pleasures of casual companionship, suggesting that intimacy is only legitimate when sanctified by marital vows, and encourages distrust of other relationships the alluring quality of which is but a ruse or a mask for secondary motivations. It encourages divisions between the sexes, telling men to be suspicious of women, for women are willing to lie about their sexual motivations, yet will in turn blame men for these prevarications. At the same time, it encourages women to be suspicious of men, telling them that men who seem committed and honest, who are, indeed, perfectly happy, may nevertheless not be above temptation, temptations that can lead to catastrophic unrest. It tells couples that they need to take their spouses to a terrifying film in order to ensure their fidelity, and that a scared spouse is more important than a satisfied one. Doubting spontaneity, the film disabuses viewers of the idea that life can be mercurial, or that people can take actions on a whim without penalizing consequence.

Fatal Attraction's treatment of sexuality can thus be viewed, in short, as advocating a world order that is distrustful, unforgiving, and resolutely privatistic. While the film energized spectators who found pleasure in its morality tale, and may have used the film to shame and scare partners into toeing the sexual line, the film's admittedly highly successful attempt at sexual disciplining nevertheless loses something profound in the process, for it advances the ultimately painful and demoralizing message that, if you take risks, you may risk losing everything you know and love. While the film was then rightly appreciated as a rejoinder to sexual dalliance, more frightening perhaps is the way it cultivates a widespread ethos of fear and suspicion. Indeed, the world order of *Fatal Attraction* suggests a profound sense of disbelief in the world, in people, and in spontaneous action. We are better left with the people with whom we are familiar, it says, rather than the ones who we may find ourselves drawn to without reason. At base, the film mounts an almost xenophobic defense against difference, arguing that the unknown is to be feared, distrusted, and armed against. In the next chapter, we will look at the ways in which the toxicity of such a position, of a reductive, us-against-them worldview, has come to be an organizing framework for feminist debates in the present day.

Chapter 5

Female Identities and Postfeminist Paradigms

In a moment of pathetic humor whose tenor would become the stock in trade of chick flicks for years onward, *Bridget Jones's Diary* (2001) features a scene where its eponymous heroine watches *Fatal Attraction* after a humiliating rejection by the caddish Daniel (Hugh Grant). Defeated and dejected, Bridget (Renée Zellweger) reposes on her couch with a cigarette in her hand and a look of exasperation on her face, watching the paradigmatic moment where Alex utters the words dreaded by every other thirtysomething singleton with marital and/ or reproductive aspirations: "I'm 36 years old, it may be my last chance to have a child." In the time warp of *Bridget Jones*, the next shot Bridget sees is Alex getting shot, her chest pierced by bullet wounds. The splicing of these two scenes and their momentary but highly suggestive appearance in the popular 2001 chick flick illustrates perhaps *Fatal Attraction*'s greatest contribution to postfeminist understandings of feminine identities: framing Alex as a cautionary figure, the film focalizes Bridget's marital and reproductive anxieties through the phantasmagoria of a desperate working woman, one whose desires both echo and serve as an ironic counterpoint to Bridget's. *Fatal Attraction*'s cameo appearance in *Bridget Jones's Diary* functions, indeed, like single women's camp; viewed from the vantage point of almost a decade and a half later, Alex's plight seems at once humorous and yet also creepily prescient.

If the fictionalized Bridget's viewing habits are to be believed, the specter of *Fatal Attraction* has had a lasting impact on contemporary understandings of singlehood, work, marriage, motherhood, and the

"It may be my last chance to have a child"; Bridget fears a similar fate awaits her.

agonized "work–life" balance, all of which are sources of exploration for this chapter. To say that *Fatal Attraction* has left an imprint on the staging of gender debates in the decades since its release is first to acknowledge the punishing function that the film has had and continues to play in publicizing the famous "biological clock," an imperative that apparently refuses to wait while women's personal lives catch up with their reproductive requirements. In this, *Fatal Attraction* has succeeded in creating a figure whose wrath is paralleled only by her sense of temporal urgency; Alex confirms, in short, the idea that relational aspirations and disappointments are felt so acutely by women as to turn their lives into a voracious hunt for companionship.

Marriage Panic

In postfeminist culture, Alex has come to characterize the unmarried working woman to such an extent that even figures who share little in common with Alex understand their plight as a response to, or in dialogue with, her image.[1] As Angela McRobbie writes of Alex, she has "entered the popular imagination of younger women as someone they must avoid ever becoming in their pursuit of independence alongside love, sex, marriage and motherhood" (2008: 39). As McRobbie's comments indicate, postfeminist culture consumes itself with the question of how independence and especially professional success can coexist with more traditional aspirations toward marriage and motherhood. If Alex's now legendary desperation answered the question of whether women can it have "it all" with a resounding "no," female mass media outlets grapple daily with the legacy that this denial has wrought. A spectral figure in female popular culture, Alex lives in perpetuity as an unfortunate woman who does not secure a companion (all the good ones are married, she laments), who longs for intimacy, and who covets the lives that other women lead. *Bridget Jones's Diary*'s invocation of *Fatal Attraction* makes overt the extent to which the fear of this eventuality agonizes young women and organizes their emotional lives, acknowledging Alex as one who gives name, shape, and substance to the shadowy anxiety of "what will happen" to women if they reach their late thirties *sans* a husband or child. Yet, while Bridget dialogues openly with this anxiety and makes fun of it in the process, more often, this haunting takes places in the margins or intertextualities of female popular culture. Trace evidence of this dialogue can be found, for instance, in an advertising tag line for Candace Bushnell's *Sex in the City* volume which reads, "these glamorous, rebellious, crazy single women, too close to forty, who are trying hard not to turn from the Audrey Hepburn of *Breakfast at Tiffany's* into the Glenn Close of *Fatal Attraction* are – still – looking for love." Marking the spectrum from desirable to desperate through the reference points of *Breakfast at Tiffany's* (1961) and *Fatal Attraction*, this tagline clearly reads the heroines of *Sex in the City* as women who battle fictionalized demons such as Alex as they execute this "search."[2]

As the professionally successful but often interpersonally challenged women of postfeminist culture confirm, the aspiration of being fabulous, strong, and professionally independent is counterposed with the desire to secure a heterosexual partnership, and often their successful coexistence is deemed both unlikely and unrealistic.

The paradigmatic image of the desperate woman.

Accordingly, postfeminst culture repeatedly reminds women that the steepest challenge they face is accessing personal and relational opportunities, a situation often causally assumed to be stymied by professional triumphs. Alex's legacy is to have provided a face and name for the articulation of the fear that having a successful career makes one unmarriageable; as well, as explored in Chapter Three, this figure was thought to offer symbolic confirmation that working too hard, or too ambitiously, lessens one's chances at finding (and retaining) romantic relationships. Though *Newsweek*'s dire predictions of the chances of marriage after the age of 30 have now been roundly debunked, they were nevertheless for years taken as "fact" and widely circulated in female popular culture even after their veracity was disputed. In *Sleepless in Seattle* (1993), for instance, a female character quotes the sentiment that "it's easier to be killed by a terrorist than it is to find a husband over the age of 40!" Though Annie (Meg Ryan) promptly corrects her, "That statistic is not true!" Annie's protest carries little reassurance because the emotional resonance of this notion has come to be more valid than its statistical accuracy. As Becky (Rosie O'Donnell) voices: "That's right, it's not true. But it feels true."

Such dialogue confirms how conversant unmarried professional women since *Fatal Attraction* tend to be with the notion that marital economies grow scarcer the longer a woman waits to partake of them. Yet, rarely acknowledged in such conversations is the fact that Alex contributed to *creating* the reality she is credited with *reflecting*. Her widely publicized image succeeded in concretizing the fear that unmarried women are doomed to spinsterhood, in a sense confirming a hypothesis that was, in truth, only speculatory. Alex and popular culture existed in a mutually parasitic relationship in the 1980s, wherein her presence codified an anxiety that became all the more real, and indeed, all the more concerning, as a result of her appearance on the popular culture landscape. The fact that the marriage "drought" was later debunked reveals the specious nature of using Alex to evidence this marital shortage, and yet her status as the main symptom for this diagnosis continues largely uninterrupted. Reading the visuals of "Single, Female, and Desperate No More," the 2006 *New York Times* piece that covered the retraction of the *Newsweek* marriage panic story confirms precisely such a system of invention, for while *Newsweek* chose to flank its article with photos of older couples who married and reproduced later in life, the *New York Times* story is accompanied by a picture of Alex, scowling in her sheer negligee. While the content of "Single, Female, and Desperate No More" realizes the promise of its title by outing the figure of the desperate, unhappy career woman as an exaggeration, the choice of this picture backhandedly confirms that Alex returns from the repressed even at the very moment her demographic reality is being disputed. In short, despite the lack of sociocultural evidence for her position, to borrow from the rhetoric of *Sleepless in Seattle*, Alex still *feels* true.

Alex's legacy in many ways continues to subtend stories of nuptial calculation, products which continue to appear as recently as the March 2008 issue of the *Atlantic Monthly* wherein contributor Lori Gottlieb argued that women in their late twenties and early thirties should settle for whatever husband they can find. As she rationalized, although their impulse might be to hold out for Mr. Right, such a decision too actively risks singlehood in one's forties.[3] Any husband, she argues, is better than no husband. That articles such as Gottlieb's continue to be heralded as *zeitgeist* statements confirms the symbolic power that the marital economy still wields over women. More potently, it suggests the continued popularity of conversations that frame unmarried women as deficient, positing them as a class that must rouse to action – and do so before it is too late – if they have any hopes of securing for themselves a connubial future.

Postfeminist Heroines, Choice, and the Danger of Anger

All the same, postfeminist representational tropes have significantly shifted the presentation of the unmarried woman. Writing in 1988 about the anxiety fueling the creation of characters like Alex, Janet Karsten Larson proposed that recent films have "begun to evidence fear of single professional women as a class" (1988: 83). In some ways, the years have been kinder to this figure than Larson predicts, for Alex has been modified in the present to the girlish, whimsical heroine who, though she feels marital pressures acutely, is nevertheless more likely to greet this challenge by purchasing a pair of stilettos than by grabbing a steak knife. While *Fatal Attraction*'s Alex seemed to offer capitalist culture only a terrorizing figure in need of eradication, unmarried professional women are actively targeted as a powerful market demographic. In this, the single professional woman anxious about her marital and reproductive prospects is more often a figure of solicitation than vilification, and entire cottage industries such as chick flicks, chick lit, and primetime female-centered television dramas court her attention. Urban single women, as inculcated especially by franchises such as *Sex and the City* and *Bridget Jones's Diary*, have been folded into a capitalist economy precisely because their cosmopolitanism and professionalization affords them some capacity for material accumulation. Yet, this acceptance is always and immediately counteracted by the notion that something in a woman's life is lacking if she is without a male partner. As Diane Negra reminds us, "postfeminism might be seen as particularly punishing in its relation to single women, having raised their cultural profile though without any corresponding enlargement of their status/options" (2008: 10). As Negra's comments indicate, though postfeminist products have made the single woman a more common figure in the media landscape, they have not significantly altered the terms on which she appears there. In fact, such products frequently manufacture the same relational anxieties that they then answer, in a feedback loop fueled by the ever-present "carrot" of marriage.

As well, though the single woman appears more frequently in female popular culture, the price of having shed her stigmatized identity is a forfeiture of indignation or anger. Specifically, though she is often wistful or neurotic, she seems no longer capable or interested in verbalizing observations that might in any way change the status quo. Created as a figure lacking the capacity for strong negative emotion, the postfeminist heroine turns a blind eye to the recognition that patriarchal ideals fuel the pressure on women to marry and reproduce, thus sweeping away potentially feminist insights in a tide of pastel purses and martini glasses. The prototypical postfeminist heroine is both unassuming and sweet, attributes that have proven so pleasurably palatable to audiences that numerous actresses not only adopt them but so do through multiple films. The girl-next-door persona shapes the star images of many successful actresses appearing in romantic comedies in the 1990s and 2000s, including Sandra Bullock (*Hope Floats, While You Were Sleeping, Two Weeks Notice*), Reese Witherspoon (*Down Home Alabama, Legally Blond, Legally Blond 2*), Kate Hudson (*How to Lose a Guy in 10 Days, Raising Helen, Fool's Gold*) and Katherine Heigl (*Knocked Up, 27 Dresses*). In each instance, the woman's charm derives largely from the fact that they are kind and unthreatening, personality traits that also guarantee their romantic pursuits a satisfying outcome. (Again, because anger might taint one's chances in a competitive marital and reproductive economy, the sweet naïf is typically more likely to couple than is the cynical best friend.)

The reverse of the compliant heroine is the selfish nemesis, a woman who tends to be vilified as "crazy." Perhaps the most distressing instance of such a characterization can be found in the casting of Jane Fonda (whose public feminism has long informed her star image) as Jennifer Lopez's shrewish mother in-law-to-be in the misogynistically titled *Monster-in-Law* (2005). If the angry feminist is now a figure meant to be rejected and lampooned, such attributions succeed in rendering those who challenge gender iniquity, and their message itself, anachronistic and reactionary. In turn, the feminist's (apparently justifiable) public flogging confirms that feminist grievances were and continue to be excessive and overstated. The contrast between the charming waif and the demanding shrew provides an explanatory framework for mass culture's turn to the impish heroine, who, it appears, is constructed out of a gesture of disavowal that implicitly accepts Alex's brand of violent resistance as abrasive, over-blown, and downright ugly.

The celebration of non-threatening women in the years since *Fatal Attraction* confirms that the need to disavow Alex's legacy organizes postfeminist life; engaged in a shadow boxing match with unseemly shrews constructed as vitriolic extremists, today's female identificatory figures cannot risk the designation of undesirability that accompanies the accusation that one is an "angry" feminist. Such commonplaces have surely limited the parameters of available feminine identities in the twenty-first century, yet this absence is typically papered over in the language of "choice," which is now a regulation element of all conversa-tions pertaining to women's lives. In fact, the idea that women must choose and then must live with those choices is an overarching ethos of the postfeminist period. Troubling about this idea, of course, is the shrinking of available discourses to include only the terms of neoliberal personal responsibility, the implication being that no matter what hap-pens to a woman, the outcome is of her choosing. While it seems hasty to credit one film with what is surely a larger rhetorical commonplace, *Fatal Attraction*'s sense that there are only a limited number of available identities from which women must choose, and indeed, that the price of making the wrong choice is dangerously steep, has proved nonetheless a highly alluring schema. As feminist critic Bonnie Dow argued:

> Postfeminism is an attempt … to take the political and make it personal, to deny that feminism has a social and political claim to make, asserting instead that woman's fate is entirely in her own hands. This illusion of agency is a seductive one, especially when the women who lose, who make bad choices, who fail to enter the market at the right time or in the right way, are terrifying and crazy, like Alex Forrest. (2006: 127)

In such a paradigm, as explored in Chapter Three, Alex emerges as one who bears sole responsibility for her bad choices, and neither the film text nor the popular reception of it bother to inquire why one must so readily accept the assumption that these choices ensure her continued singlehood. Why is it so easy, for instance, to believe Alex when she matter of factly states that this is her "last chance" at motherhood? Why must we frame marital and reproductive economies as premised on tenets of scarcity, whereby people are given a limited number of chances that they must take, or risk forfeiting their participation altogether? I do not mean to say that biological realities do not impinge on this discussion, but rather that the temporal constraints touted by postfeminist culture have an unforgivingly narrow timeline, such that if a woman is neither pregnant nor married at 36, it seems perfectly reasonable to say that she will likely never be either. And, despite the public renunciation of this idea and the fact that women daily prove this to be untrue, this legend continues to be circulated as fact.

Postfeminist Catfights

Part of the reason that *Fatal Attraction* could so glibly reinforce marital and reproductive panic and in turn stand as an exemplar of such pressures is that it had the perfect foil for Alex in Beth, a woman who did make the "right" choices, and whose generally contented life reflects the prudence of having done so. More than a battle between the sexes, the film shrewdly isolates its focus to a battle between Alex and Beth, the career woman versus the traditional mother, a reductive oversimplification that nevertheless seems to have codified female identities in the present era.[4] Put simply, *Fatal Attraction* takes the foremost two pressures facing the postfeminist subject, career and family, and separates them into two different figures. While the rhetoric of "having it all" attempts to reconcile these supposedly opposing poles, *Fatal Attraction* refuses to principally parse out this issue, any responsible treatment of which needs to think about the role that men and public systems of support (or lack thereof) have in making the coexistence of career and family commitments either viable or not. Instead, using the unflaggingly individualist, neoliberal logic detailed in Chapter Four, the film abdicates responsibility for thinking about this issue as one which women and families face as a collective. Instead, by framing the debate as the career woman versus the traditional mother, the film insists that these must be mutually exclusive identities and interrogates female life choices on these grounds. While this reductive oversimplification seems almost laughably facile and hence hardly worthy of being afforded credence in the discourse of feminist concern, this question has become the premier women's issue of our time.

To understand this process, one must first take for granted the notion that the mass media have increasingly become the vehicle by which feminist agendas are not only publicized, but also organized, so that the terms of any debate are more likely to be set by popular culture than by committed activists. Accordingly, the foremost feminist item to have consumed air and print space in the past five years is the "stay-at-home versus working mother" conflict, a conversation instigated in part by Lisa Belkin's "Opt-Out Revolution" piece in the *New York Times* in 2003. Belkin's story about the ranks of privileged and successful women abandoning their high-powered careers in order to spend time with their children both sparked and legitimized a debate that exhorts women to make a "choice" between two identities, that of the ambitious career woman and that of the devoted mother. Much as Alex and Beth are cast into stock roles whereby neither is afforded full subjectivity, the conversation turns on pat images of women that have few real-life correlatives. The problems with the debate's framing are multiple; naysayers who reject this paradigm have reiterated, for instance, that the opt-out trend has been exaggerated and overinflated, others have pointed out the myopia of basing a cultural diagnosis on the actions of a few privileged women. As well, as Mary Douglas Vavrus argues, opting out stories "legitimate dangerously archaic notions about women, work and family ... opting out fits well with this conservative rhetoric by highlighting old-fashioned family arrangements, complete with heterosexual women proclaiming home and family as their rightful domain" (2007: 49–50). In the name of "exploring" options, the opt-out conversation tends to reinforce gender-specific ideals, namely by assuming parenthood is the main purview of women and knowingly recuperating new traditionalist notions of the contented housewife. The so-called "mommy wars" that have emerged in the wake of this moment are predicated on precisely such a showdown, for they suggest that women are the ones who will battle out the terms on which feminine identity will be defined, and that women's options fall neatly into these two opposing categorizations.

The legacy of the Alex verses Beth showdown has had a wide reach, thanks to its suggestion that retrograde definitions of family circumscribe the terms on which feminist debates can be premised. Scores of recent books and articles discursively confirm that the most pressing issue facing women today is this "choice," one organized by a duel embodied by Beth's and Alex's life stations. In one iteration of this conversation, contemporary women decry the deleterious effects visited upon women and society when females aspire to the mantle of "working woman"; such discourses point out the personal and communal casualties that ensue in the wake of largescale movements towards female employment.[5] In such tracts, the figure of the working woman serves as the scapegoat for social ills, and their critical focus circles around the idea that a return to traditional values would make women happier and would benefit a world that suffers as a result of female career aspirations. Such a viewpoint was evidenced, for instance, by the controversy in September 2006 when a *Forbes* online contributor wrote an article claiming that working women make bad wives. While feminist reaction to this putdown was swift, the fact that the commentator could again frame this as a battle between "work" and "wifehood" – and that his detractors were then confined to these paradigms even in their vociferous rebuttals – confirms the lasting attribution of work and wifehood as warring rather than complementary identities.

The same conclusion can be reached from the fact that women today are interpellated by a culture that asks them to justify whatever position they adopt with respect to the "work–life balance." While some women defend the decision to abandon the workplace, others either proclaim their decision to work, and/or exhort other women to realize the financial and personal risks inherent in retreat.[6] Personal accounts and polemics are joined by studies of this trend, reports which overwhelmingly note the lack of institutional or corporate support for programs that make accommodation for women and men juggling familial and professional commitments.[7] Collectively, the energy swirling around this issue suggests that we are still very

In this catfight, Alex meets her bloody fate at the hands of Beth.

much a culture made anxious by the task of negotiating female lives, perhaps in part because the reductive models by which we attempt this negotiation have left much to be desired. While the profound unease surrounding this issue manifests itself in obsessive handwringing about the cost of selecting one path at the expense of another, one cannot escape the sense that the debate is intellectually impoverished given the fact that the only way to conceive this issue has been to pit one form of womanhood against the other.

In this, *Fatal Attraction*'s scripting of Beth and Alex proved highly prescient, for Alex Forrest still serves as a cautionary figure for a very undesirable feminine identity, and her appearance, even twenty years out, ratchets up the cultural pressure on women to obsess about their life choices. While this is an important preoccupation no doubt, the fact that Dan largely drops out of the frame in the film is symptomatic of precisely the problem with current gender formats. While Dan's removal from the catfight between Beth and Alex can be argued as evidence of his ineffectuality, the fact remains that, as Bonnie Dow has remarked, "Dan doesn't get to be the hero because he is the *prize*" (2006: 126). If the fight between the women betrays itself as a battle to secure for themselves a scarce commodity, such a deficit model surely organizes the attribution that Dan is the type of man a woman should hold on to. Yet, this observation is alarming in no small part because it invokes retrograde assumptions of female dependency and at the same time grants men a pass for mistreating women. Even though Dan cheats on Beth and misuses Alex, the two women still masochistically desire his presence. As an organizational model, the film's ending betrays the extent to which postfeminist culture organizes itself around the specter of female competition and animus; the film evinces no sentiment that the women are in any way "in this together."

Instead, just as Dan remains outside the frame of the fight and later the murder, so too are men largely absent from the "mommy wars," conversations which generally fail to note the role that male prerogatives might take in adding a third or fourth term to this reductive binary. Easier, it seems, is to avoid men, who are obviated in a sensationalized display that prefers to see the problems facing women as imaginatively resolvable by beating up another woman. Refusing consideration of the political, institutional, or economic determinants that impinge on female lives – pressures that in many ways render the concept of "choice" a misnomer – models such as the one offered in *Fatal Attraction* oversimplify and personalize a debate that is anything but. The beloved catfights we have come to associate with considerations of female lives are hardly responsible representations of what are legitimate fractures in feminist theorization; rather, they exhibit a likemindedness with *Fatal Attraction*'s gratuitous ending in that they too pander to longstanding audience bias and safely reassure onlookers of the battle's easy reduction and pat solutions. To frame the debate in this way betrays the fact that questions about the content of, and decision making in, female lives are still viewed as generally inconsequential. To refuse the matter true consideration and acknowledge the complexities therein is in fact a show of neglect mystified by the plethora of popular attention afforded this issue. Although prettied up in spectacle, contemporary conversation on the status of female lives outs itself as having much in common with *Fatal Attraction*'s sensationalized conclusion – both offer little except easy answers, answers that disappoint in their willingness to reduce female identities to caricature and competition. Calls for meaningful communication and coalition amongst women, and the insistence that this debate be reframed in ways that take into account economic and institutional determinants, thus perhaps need the same sort of urgency and indignation that is, in fact, Alex's stock in trade. Perhaps, indeed, it is time for feminists who desire a debate reformulated on premises of inclusion rather that exclusion to demand the same sort of attention that Alex did, to say collectively that, in our demand for coalition rather than competition, *we* will not be ignored.

Notes

Notes to Chapter 1

1　In one of the film's more obvious goofs, Beth identifies her daughter as being 6, while Dan refers to her as 5.

2　Susan Faludi quotes a slightly different line on this same topic; in this interview, Lyne says of the apartments, "They were a little sad, if you want me to be honest. They lacked soul" (1988: 49).

3　In his director's commentary, Lyne describes how he intentionally kept the film's colors muted and recounts how in the scene where Dan drives out of the city in a rental car, the vehicle delivered to the film set was red. Because his use of red is sporadic yet deliberate, Lyne insisted that they change it.

4　Dearden was of course not the first filmmaker to exploit the terrifying immediacy of the phone in his work. Notable cinematic entries into the annals of telephonic terror include *Heard Over the Phone* (1909), *Call Northside 777* (1947), *Sorry, Wrong Number* (1948), *Southside 1-1000* (1950), *Dial M for Murder* (1954), *I Saw What You Did* (1965), *When a Stranger Calls* (1979), *Scream* (1996), and *Phonebooth* (2003).

5　Family photos are another prevailing motif in the film; framed photos of the Gallaghers are shown repeatedly in Dan's office as well as strewn throughout the Gallaghers' family condo and later their country home. Of course, the most famous photo moment is the film's last shot, which is explored in Chapter Two.

6　The film also not so subtly uses this call to suggest that Alex's culinary talents tend toward the murderous. Alex tries to cajole Dan to spend the day with her, and by way of explaining that he is already multiply overcommitted, Dan says he has not eaten, and he has to take the dog for a walk. Alex tellingly replies, "Well, bring the dog. I love animals. I'm a great cook."

7 Alex also makes a tape of herself talking which Dan listens to as he drives, a maneuver that metonymically forces upon Dan a *completed* call, in response to the dozens of others he refuses to take.

8 Notably, Alex is not the only one who cross-pollinates. By bringing his dog Quincy into Alex's apartment Dan has also facilitated this swap, although he seems oblivious to the fact that by recreating his own cozy family scene in Alex's space, he has further heightened her hopes that he will allow such recreations in the future.

9 Dan's intrusions into Alex's life are all similarly futile. Though he too breaks into Alex's apartment in order to search for proof of the falsity of Alex's pregnancy, he never finds it. Likewise, she tends to treat all of his visits, even those wherein he demands that she leave him alone, as proof of his commitment to her.

10 Rabbits too have a historical link to issues of fertility. A pregnancy detection method, the now obsolete "rabbit test" promises that if a woman is pregnant and she injects her blood into a rabbit, the rabbit will die. This legend was gender bent and lampooned in the critically panned comedy *Rabbit Test* (1978), which features Billy Crystal as a pregnant man. Less idiosyncratically, rabbits tend to be associated with rapid copulation and reproduction.

11 Alex's drowning and resurfacing attack quote *Diabolique* (1955), a film wherein the supposedly dead husband rises up from a bathtub, in turn shocking his wife to her death.

12 The attack itself also seems to quote *Psycho* since Alex comes after Beth with a large knife, and aggressively slashes through the shower curtains, *à la* Normal Bates. Likewise, as in Hitchcock's film, red blood stripes the walls and floors following Alex's death.

Notes to Chapter 2

1 In some ways, the film owes its greatest debt to Clint Eastwood's *Play Misty for Me* (1971). Eastwood also stars in the film and he plays Dave Garber, a San Francisco DJ who sleeps with, and then finds himself stalked by, a vicious and unpredictable woman, Evelyn, a recurring caller to his show. In both large- and small-scale comparisons, *Fatal Attraction* shares much with *Play Misty for Me*. Evelyn, like Alex, is quick to violent anger, slits her wrists in a desperate please for attention, repeatedly comes over to Dave's house unannounced, terrorizes him using the phone, and offers to be his Madame Butterfly. She stalks his longtime girlfriend, Tobie, brutally attacks his African-American maid, and in the film's climax, is revealed to be posing as

Tobie's roommate. Like Alex, Evelyn eventually meets a bloody fate, when she is pushed off the balcony of Tobie's beachside home and falls over a cliff.

2   Sherry Lansing, the film's producer, publicly expressed her confusion over Alex's excoriation by audiences. Although the authenticity of such statements is difficult to believe, Lansing repeatedly said that she respected Alex as a woman willing to stand up for herself, and felt that Alex had been "sadly misunderstood" (quoted in Mass, 1987–8: 32). Glenn Close also claims to have felt sympathy for her character: in a 1988 interview she told Barbara Walters, "I always thought of her as being tragic rather than evil."

3   Careful observers will notice that Dan is also often filmed through windows and glass. However, in these scenes the camera is generally watching Dan from afar, such as when it spies on him surreptitiously entering Alex's apartment building, or reacting to the sight of his acid-laden car. Although these stylized devices typically put a momentary distance between Dan and the viewer, their inclusion seems predominantly aesthetic.

4   Admittedly, the most straightforward interpretation of this scene sees it as offering a vision of the family's reconstitution. Feminist critic Ellen Willis reads the film ironically, however, because, as she says, the harmonious image comes out of nowhere after 90 minutes of angst, terror, and mayhem.

5   Ansen insists on *Fatal Attraction*'s designation as a horror film, comparing it to *Repulsion* (1965), *Friday the 13th* (1980), and *Nightmare on Elm Street* (1984).

6   Supporting the idea that Alex is ever present, Judith Williamson notes that the roving handheld camera outside the Gallaghers' country home could be read as her point of view, just as the horror films uses similar camera work to invoke the presence of the monster who hovers around the house about to be attacked (1993: 67).

7   Linda Ruth Williams also obliquely references the idea that the Medusa's gaze incapacitates Dan, for she describes him as "afflicted by a certain blindness" thanks to his encounters with Alex (2005: 184). Williams continues, "Because he is Alex's visual prey he often cannot see her – he cannot look back. She chooses him, pinning him with her gaze first erotically and then aggressively, seeing him before he sees her, peeping through the windows of his life" (2005: 184).

8   Chapter Four will take up this suggestive paradox, whereby a film apparently so invested in Reagan era family values nevertheless has little compunction about endorsing abortion when the child is not the product of the nuclear family.

9   Barry Keith Grant makes a similar claim, reading Alex as the return of Dan's "repressed dissatisfaction with his marriage" (2004: 159).

10   The film frequently uses its mise en scène to associate Alex with a somewhat exoticized otherness, since Dan meets Alex at a Japanese sushi restaurant, and goes dancing with her at a salsa club. Both locales obliquely speak to the ways in which the affair unmoors Dan from his white bourgeois life.

11   We might, however, read the sequence where Dan plays Alex's tape in the darkened attic as a noir confession scene, since he hovers around the tape, in shadows, listening to her call him cowardly. Yet, even here he has not come to answer for his crimes but more to hide the evidence of them. Dan is visibly startled, for instance, when Beth suddenly taps him on the shoulder, an interruption meant to signal not merely Beth's encroaching wrath, but Alex's as well.

12   A shot of the fan also introduces the scene where Dan and Alex lie in bed following their Sunday night tryst, although this time the fan is still.

13   Alex's violent streak has also been credited to psychological factors, and she is sometimes cited as an example of borderline personality disorder. While this designation has proved useful for clinicians, when examined in the context of the noir, Alex's behavior seems less idiosyncratic. Indeed, the femme fatale often exhibits antisocial tendencies.

14   Sarah Harwood inventively postulates that what Dan desires is Alex's silence, as evidenced by the fact that he puts his hands around her throat. Harwood writes, "Alex's speech must be repressed ... as he strangles her, we have an extraordinary subjective shot of Dan's face from Alex's point of view. His face is so twisted with venom and hatred that it is almost unrecognizable" (1997: 119).

15   It seems fitting to end a chapter on genre hybridity with a discussion of the erotic thriller, which is by nature a hybrid genre in itself. As Linda Ruth Williams argues, the erotic thriller bleeds into and out of adjacent forms such as the classic noir, neo-noir, porn, woman's films, serial killer and horror films (2005: 26).

Notes to Chapter 3

1   Audiences made their intentions toward Alex's fate well known by offering a chorus of running commentary. While "Kill the bitch" was supposedly the most popular refrain, Faludi quotes additional zingers such as, "Do it, Michael. Kill her already" and "Punch the bitch's face in" (1991: 112). Further proof of the emotional storm unleashed by Alex was offered by director Adrian Lyne, who bragged that he had taped shrill audiences passionately denouncing the female lead.

2   Twenty years later *Newsweek* boldly retracted that statement, adorning the cover of their June 5, 2006 issue with the conciliatory line, "Why We Were Wrong."

3   The age of 36 seems to be particularly perilous for cinematic American women, perhaps because it is assumed that by this point women's reproductive capacities phase into a period of sharp decline. The unnamed heroine of *Rebecca* (1940) promises her prospective husband "never to be thirty-six years old."

4   The idea that single women manage personal disappointments by attempting to steal an attached woman's life and/or family was similarly echoed in *Single White Female* (1992) and *The Hand That Rocks the Cradle* (1992). These tracts frame women who regularly enjoy masculine companionship and/or have children as objects of envy, and verifies the assumption that not having access to such relations can turn unattached women crazy.

5   In James Dearden's original screenplay, Beth was a teacher who had taken time off to raise her daughter, but was now planning to return to work. *Fatal Attraction*'s recasting of her as a stay-at-mother without any apparent career aspirations (or evidence that she possessed such aspirations in the past) fueled the perception that the film drew strict and permanent lines between stay-at-home women and those who labor outside the home.

6   A shot of Reagan giving this speech was also included in the AMC television show, *Movies That Shook the World*, during its discussion of the feminist debates surrounding *Fatal Attraction*.

7   While many feminists found the film distressing in that it so clearly sides with supposedly victimized men, others found themselves intoxicated by such a powerful portrayal of female anger. Comparing Alex with the biblical Lilith, the vixen who unleashed 500 demons, Karen Durbin gleefully contends that both representations acknowledge "a guilty, fearful male fantasy that you can't keep a good woman down all the time … if they embody male fear, they also acknowledge female rage" (1987: 90).

8   The problem of Dan's likeability was indeed a major stumbling block for the film, since Dearden's protagonist in *Diversion*, Guy, on whom Dan is based, was a serial adulterer with little respect for women. As Joyce Thompson explains, industry executives rejected the film on this basis, and Paramount CEO Michael Eisner initially passed on *Fatal Attraction* because he felt that Dan was not sympathetic enough.

9   Lyne also eagerly identified places in the film where he modeled the Gallaghers' behaviors and surroundings on the dynamics of his own family, thus testifying to his desire to make this domestic unit seem as "common" or "normal" as possible.

10   That Close would be cast as such a woman is not as inevitable as it would seem today. In films such as *The World According to Garp* (1982), *The Big Chill* (1983), and *The Natural* (1985), Close played characters that were angelic, maternal, and principled, and she was largely typecast as a woman who inspired rather than terrorized men. Her role as a defense attorney in *Jagged Edge* (1985), however, comes closer to the Alex figure, since she appears as a lonely divorcee so desperate for male companionship that she repeatedly sleeps with her client, a man accused of brutally murdering his wife. In this part, Close appears so crippled by her sexual and emotional needs so as not to notice that her lover is a killer. *Fatal Attraction*'s producers nevertheless still doubted that Close could be ruthless or evil enough to play Alex, and Close had to zealously pursue the part. Notably, star discourses narrating the audition process imbue Close with a sense of singlemindedness that is Alex-worthy, since the press reported that she secured the role as a result of her ambition and determination.

11   Like Douglas' image as the "everyman," Close's portrayal of a vengeful career woman has in many ways come to be the definitive moment of her career. Subsequent to this role, Close appeared as the treacherous Marquise de Merteuil in *Dangerous Liaisons* (1988) and the wicked, puppy-killing Cruella de Vil in *101 Dalmatians* (1996) and *102 Dalmatians* (2000). Close's budding television career has also capitalized on her image as a woman who flirts with the law, both in a season-long guest appearance as police captain Monica Rawling on *The Shield* (2004–5) and as the unscrupulous lawyer Patty Hewes in *Damages* (2007–).

12   The original ending for *Double Indemnity*, a classic noir film from which *Fatal Attraction* borrows both visuals and themes, also ended on a similarly brutal note. In this scene Walter Neff enters the gas chamber to face his death, as punishment for killing the husband of his lover Phyllis.

13   The film was released in Japan with this ending, though American theaters only carried the reshot version.

14   This sense that audiences could not have abided by the original ending was also echoed in reviews. Though critical of the artistic value of the revised last scenes, the *New Yorker*'s David Denby justified the alteration by explaining that audiences needed "a release from the burden of caring for an exasperating woman" (118).

15   Glenn Close apparently fought hard not to change the original ending, and has subsequently gone on record with her opinion that it was a total violation of Alex's character. Close says she never saw Alex as a homicidal woman, and felt that turning her into one made Alex a "one-note" character. Close even initially refused to shoot the alternate ending, but was eventually persuaded to do so.

Notes to Chapter 4

1   Descriptions of such events can be found in Corliss (1987), Nadelson (1988), and Schickel (1987).

2   Though both these examples deal explicitly with sexual danger, the film also includes footage of a news cast where then-Mayor Ed Koch refers to the "atrocious" crimes committed by three men with what looks like an electrode. This inclusion identifies New York City in the 1980s as a lawless battleground, an attribution that works to justify Beth's desire to move to the suburbs and identifies the inhabitants of the city as multiply imperiled.

3   Robin Wood has argued that numerous 1980s films construct the adult spectator as a child, especially those that answer infantile demands for scenarios that involve danger but nevertheless always lead the child/adult safely "home."

4   This alignment between sex and danger is perhaps the foremost animating principle of the erotic thriller, a genre for which *Fatal Attraction* is considered foundational.

5   Andrews recalls the police officer's quip to Dan that he has made his bed, and now needs to lie in it. Observing that the majority of the film is dedicated to the consequences of Dan's affair, Andrews creatively argues that said bed figures "as the entire narrative framework" (2006: 64).

6   The spectacle of the crying child in this scene is surely one of the reasons reviewers accused *Fatal Attraction* of crass manipulation; as David Andrews acknowledges, "the presence of a child – the ever proscriptive Young Person – is in the erotic thriller a more reliable predictor of a guilt-ridden trajectory than the presence of a spouse alone" (2006: 64).

7   This discussion clearly borrows logic from the psychosexual dynamics explored in Hitchcock's *Rear Window*. As well, *Fatal Attraction* has drawn comparison to *Vertigo* (1958), another film consumed with the sexual politics of looking. See Corliss (1987).

8   That the film would introduce abortion at all is nonetheless striking from the perspective of twenty years hence. Though the repressive cultural climate of "family values" that characterizes the United States in the early twenty-first century is in many ways remarkably akin to the late 1980s, abortion seems to have significantly abated as an option in mass cultural discourse. In 2007, for instance, a rash of fertility comedies (*Waitress, Knocked Up*, and *Juno*) featured women facing unplanned pregnancies, yet none of them weighed abortion with any real consideration.

9   The inconvenience of taking Alex's pregnancy seriously, I suspect, informed speculations on the part of the critics and fans that she was not "really"

pregnant. Despite a doctor's confirmation of the pregnancy's veracity, spectators continued to doubt that Alex was telling Dan the truth. Though she is admittedly troubled, Alex's treatment in this regard nevertheless reflects a patriarchal prerogative that would rather assume she is lying than deal with a difficult reality.

10   Dan also blithely and repeatedly denies he has any knowledge of family law, a branch of law that deals with nevertheless similar principles in that it scrutinizes familial relationships, often in crisis, to decide issues of ownership and care. Thus, even *this* disavowal can be taken as evidence of his professional insufficiencies.

Notes to Chapter 5

1   Amy Taubin's comments on the film suggest that this fear organized even her initial viewing of *Fatal Attraction* in 1987. She confesses, "my immediate response to the film was not so much to identify with Alex as to be terrified that others might spot a resemblance between us. I know that a despairing phone call does not inevitably lead to boiled bunnies, kidnapped children, and cut-up wives … But I've known men who responded to such a call as if it were a knife. And I was humiliated to think they could use *Fatal Attraction* to support their belief that I was crazy" (1987: 90).

2   In another key moment of intertextuality, in one episode of the television series *Sex and the City* Samantha relocates to the meatpacking district of Manhattan. Though this move recalls Alex's neighborhood, by the late 1990s the district was more chic than abject.

3   Gottlieb references not *Fatal Attraction* but *Broadcast News* (1987), another paradigmatic example of a professional woman's failures on the marriage market.

4   For a discussion of how the perception of scarcity in the marital economy leads to troubling cycles of jealousy and divisiveness between women, see my article "Marriage Envy" (Leonard, 2006).

5   See especially Crittenden (2000) and O'Beirne (2006).

6   For a rather sanctimonious defense of opting out, see Flanagan (2006). For a reading which looks at the culture of motherhood as manifesting a self-justifying ethos which purposefully turns it into a full time job, see Warner (2006). For texts that urge women to work for both personal and economic reasons, see Hirschman (2006) and Bennetts (2007).

7   For studies of this issue, see Stone (2007) and Hewlett (2007).

Works Cited

Andrews, David. 2006. "Sex Is Dangerous, So Satisfy Your Wife: The Softcore Thriller in Its Contexts." *Cinema Journal* 45.3 (Spring): 59–89.

Ansen, David. 1987. "Nightmare on Madison Avenue." *Newsweek* (28 September): 76.

Babener, Liahna. 1992. "Patriarchal Politics in *Fatal Attraction*." *Journal of Popular Culture* 26.3 (Winter): 25–34.

Belkin, Lisa. 2003. "The Opt-out Revolution." *New York Times Magazine* (26 October): 42.

Bennetts, Leslie. 2007. *The Feminine Mistake: Are We Giving Up Too Much?* New York: Voice.

Berland, Elaine, and Wechter, Marilyn. 1992. "Fatal/Fetal Attraction: Psychological Aspects of Imagining Female Identity in Contemporary Film." *Journal of Popular Culture* 26.3 (Winter): 35–45.

Bromley, Susan, and Hewitt, Pamela. 1992. "*Fatal Attraction*: The Sinister Side of Women's Conflict about Career and Family." *Journal of Popular Culture* 26.3 (Winter): 17–23.

Bruning, Fred. 1987. "Sex and the Psychopath Factor." *Maclean's* (23 November): 7.

Canby, Vincent. 1988. "Our Big Hits: Out of This World." *The New York Times* (31 January), late ed., sec. 2: 19+.

Close, Glenn. 1988. Interview with Barbara Walters. *Barbara Walters Special*. ABC. 11 April.

Conlon, James. 1996. "The Place of Passion: Reflections on *Fatal Attraction*." *The Dread of Difference*. Ed. Barry Keith Grant. Austin: University of Texas Press, 401–11.

Copjec, Joan. 1993. "The Phenomenal Nonphenomenal: Private Space in Film Noir." *Shades of Noir*. Ed. Joan Copjec. London: Verso, 167–97.

Corliss, Richard. 1987. "Killer" *Time* (16 November): 72–9.

Cowie, Elizabeth. 1993. "Film Noir and Women." *Shades of Noir*. Ed. Joan Copjec. London: Verso, 121–65.

Creed, Barbara. 1993. *Horror and the Monstrous Feminine: Film, Feminism, Psychoanalysis.* New York: New York University Press.

Creed, Barbara. 1996. "Horror and the Monstrous-Feminine: An Imaginary Abjection." *The Dread of Difference.* Ed. Barry Keith Grant. Austin: University of Texas Press, 35–65.

Crittenden, Danielle. 2000. *What Our Mothers Didn't Tell Us: Why Happiness Eludes the Modern Woman.* New York: Simon and Schuster.

Derry, Charles. 2001. *The Suspense Thriller: Films in the Shadow of Alfred Hitchcock.* Jefferson, NC: McFarland.

Doane, Mary Ann. 1991. "The Moving Image: Pathos and the Maternal." *Imitations of Life: A Reader on Film and Television Melodrama.* Ed. Marcia Landy. Detroit: Wayne State University Press, 283–306.

Douglas, Mary. 1966. *Purity and Danger: An Analysis of Concepts of Pollution and Taboo.* New York: Praeger.

Dow, Bonnie J. 2006. "The Traffic in Men and the *Fatal Attraction* of Postfeminist Masculinity." *Women's Studies in Communication* 29.1 (Spring): 113–31.

Durbin, Karen. 1987. "The Cat's Meow." The Rabbit Died: Eight Capsule Comments on *Fatal Attraction. Village Voice* (15 December): 90.

Elsaesser, Thomas. 1991. "Tales of Sound and Fury: Observations on the Family Melodrama." *Imitations of Life: A Reader on Film and Television Melodrama.* Ed. Marcia Landy. Detroit: Wayne State University Press, 68–91.

Faludi, Susan. 1988. "Fatal Distortion." *Mother Jones.* (February/March): 27–30; 49–50.

Faludi, Susan. 1991. *Backlash: The Undeclared War against American Women.* New York: Anchor Books.

Flanagan, Caitlin. *To Hell with All That: Loving and Loathing Our Inner Housewife.* New York: Virago, 2006.

Friedan, Betty. 1963. *The Feminine Mystique.* New York: W. W. Norton.

Gledhill, Christine. 1999. "History of Genre Criticism." *The Cinema Book.* Eds. Pam Cook and Mieke Bernink. London: British Film Institute, 137–47.

Gottlieb, Lori. 2008. "Marry Him: The Case for Settling for Mr. Good Enough." *Atlantic Monthly* (March): 76–83.

Grant, Barry Keith. 2004. "Rich and Strange: The Yuppie Horror Film." *Planks of Reason: Essays on the Horror Film.* Ed. Barry Keith Grant and Christopher Sharret. Lanham, MD: Scarecrow Press, 153–69.

Halliday, John. 1972. *Sirk on Sirk: Interviews with Jon Halliday.* New York: Viking.

Hartford Courant. 2007. "From Bunny Boiler to Marriage Saver." AP Wire Story. *The Hartford Courant* (30 December): D2.

Harwood, Sarah. 1997. *Family Fictions: Representations of the Family in 1980s Hollywood Cinema.* New York: St. Martins.

Henricksson, Lisa. 1987. "Back to the Boudoir." *Rolling Stone* (17 December): 147–8.

Hewlett, Sylvia Ann. *Off Ramps and On Ramps: Keeping Talented Women on the Road to Success*. Boston: Harvard Business School Press, 2007.

Hirschberg, Lynn. 1987. "Adrian's Line on Sex." *Rolling Stone* (19 November): 14.

Hirschman, Linda. 2006. *Get to Work: A Manifesto for Women of the World*. New York: Viking.

Holmlund, Christine. 1994. "A Decade of Deadly Dolls: Hollywood and the Woman Killer." *Moving Targets: Women, Murder and Representation*. Ed. Helen Birch. Berkeley: University of California Press, 127–51.

Jermyn, Deborah. 1996. "Rereading the Bitches from Hell: A Feminist Appropriation of the Female Psychopath." *Screen* 37.3 (Autumn): 251–67.

Jones, Amelia. 1991. "She Was Bad News: Male Paranoia and the Contemporary New Woman." *Camera Obscura*. 25 & 26: 297–320.

Joshel, Sandra R. 1992. "Fatal Liaisons and Dangerous Attraction: The Destruction of Feminist Voices." *Journal of Popular Culture* 26.3 (Winter): 59–70.

Kael, Pauline. 1987. "The Feminine Mystique." *New Yorker* (19 October): 106–7; 109–12.

Kales, Emily Fox. 2003. "Body Double as Body Politic: Psychosocial Myth and Cultural Binary in *Fatal Attraction*." *International Journal of Psychoanalysis* 84: 1631–7.

Keesey, Douglas. 2001. "They Kill for Love: Defining the Erotic Thriller as a Film Genre." *Cineaction* (Summer): 44–53.

Klinger, Barbara. 1994. *Melodrama and Meaning: History, Culture, and the Films of Douglas Sirk*. Bloomington: Indiana University Press.

Krutnik, Frank. 1991. *In a Lonely Street: Film Noir, Genre and Masculinity*. London: Taylor and Francis.

Kunen, James. 1987. "The Dark Side of Love." *People Weekly* (26 October): 88–95.

Larson, Janet Karsten. 1988. "Filming the Poor in Spirit." *Cross Currents* 38.1 (Spring): 76–86.

Leonard, Suzanne. 2006. "Marriage Envy." *Women's Studies Quarterly*. Special Issue on Envy. Ed. Jane Gallop. 34.3 & 34.4 (Fall/Winter): 43–64.

Marcus, Daniel. 2004. *Happy Days and Wonder Years: The Fifties and Sixties in Contemporary Cultural Politics*. New Brunswick: Rutgers University Press.

Mass, Roslyn. 1987–8. "The Mirror Cracked: The Career Woman in a Trio of Lansing Films." *Film Criticism* 12.2 (Winter): 28–36.

McGinn, Daniel. 2006. "Marriage by the Numbers." *Newsweek* (5 June): 40–8.

McNair, Brian. 2002: *Striptease Culture: Sex, Media and the Democratisation of Desire*. London: Routledge.

McRobbie, Angela. 2008. *The Aftermath of Feminism*. London: Sage Press.

Mercer, John, and Shingler, Martin. 2004. *Melodrama: Genre, Style, Sensibility*. Short Cuts Series. London: Wallflower Press.

Merck, Mandy. 1988. "Bedroom Horror: The Fatal Attraction of *Intercourse.*" *Feminist Review* 30: 89–103.

Nadelson, Regina. 1988. "Fatally Yours." *Guardian* (7 January): 20.

Naremore, James. 1998. *More Than Night: Film Noir in Its Contexts*. Berkeley: University of California Press.

Negra, Diane. 2008. *What a Girl Wants?: Fantasizing the Reclamation of Self in Postfeminism*. New York: Routledge.

Nowell-Smith, Geoffrey. 1991. "Minnelli and Melodrama." *Imitations of Life: A Reader on Film and Television Melodrama*. Ed. Marcia Landy. Detroit: Wayne State University Press, 268–72.

O'Beirne, Kate. 2006. *Women Who Make the World Worse: And How Their Radical Feminist Assault Is Ruining Our Schools, Families, Military, and Workplaces*. New York: Penguin.

Pally, Marcia. 1988. "Kin Con: The Family Goes Bananas." *Film Comment* 24.1: 11–15.

Ronell, Avital. 1989. *The Telephone Book: Technology, Schizophrenia, Electric Speech*. Lincoln: University of Nebraska Press.

Sargent, Lydia. 1988. "Kill the Bitch." *Zeta* (January): 33–4.

Schickel, Richard. 1987. "The War Between the Mates." *Time* (28 September): 69.

Segal, Naomi. 1997. The Fatal Attraction of *The Piano.*" *Scarlet Letters: Fictions of Adultery from Antiquity to the 1990s*. Ed. Nicholas White and Naomi Segal. Basingstoke: Macmillan, 199–211.

Simon, John. 1987. "Overindulgence." *National Review* 39.23 (4 December): 55–60.

Stone, Laurie. 1987. "The New Femme Fatale." *Ms.* (December): 78–9.

Stone, Pamela. 2007. *Opting Out?: Why Women Really Quit Careers and Head Home*. Berkeley: University of California Press.

Tanner, Tony. 1979. *Adultery and the Novel: Contract and Transgression*. Baltimore: Johns Hopkins University Press.

Taubin, Amy. 1987. "Too Close for Comfort." The Rabbit Died: Eight Capsule Comments on *Fatal Attraction. Village Voice* (15 December): 90.

Telotte, J. P. 1989. "The Call of Desire and the Film Noir." *Literature Film Quarterly* 17.1: 50–9.

Thompson, Joyce. 1992. "From Diversion to *Fatal Attraction*: The Transformation of a Morality Play into a Hollywood Hit." *Journal of Popular Culture* 26.3 (Winter): 5–15.

Vavrus, Mary Douglas. 2007. "Opting Out Moms in the News: Selling New Traditionalism in the New Millennium." *Feminist Media Studies* 7.1: 47–63.

Warner, Judith. 2006. *Perfect Madness: Motherhood in the Age of Anxiety.* New York: Riverhead.

Westerlund-Shands, Kerstin. 1993. "Female Fatality in the Movies." *Moderna Sprak* 87.2: 113–20.

Williams, Linda. 2000. "Discipline and Fun: *Psycho* and Postmodern Cinema." *Reinventing Film Studies.* Ed. Christine Gledhill and Linda Williams. New York: Oxford University Press, 351–78.

Williams, Linda Ruth. 2005. *The Erotic Thriller in Contemporary Cinema.* Bloomington: Indiana University Press.

Williamson, Judith. 1993. "Nightmare on Madison Avenue: *Fatal Attraction.*" *Deadline at Dawn: Film Criticism 1980–1990.* New York: Marion Boyars: 65–8.

Willis, Ellen. 1987. "Sins of the Fathers." *Village Voice* (15 December): 85–6.

Wood, Robin. 1986. *Hollywood from Vietnam to Reagan.* New York: Columbia University Press.

Yellin, Jessica. 2006. "Single, Female, and Desperate No More." *New York Times* (4 June), sec. 4: 1.

Index

9½ Weeks (1986) 2, 70
101 Dalmatians (1996) 126n11
102 Dalmatians (2000) 126n11
abjection 46–7, 50, 51
abortion 48, 70, 97, 98, 102, 123n8,
    127n8
    pro-choice 98
adultery 1–2, 11, 12, 20, 21, 101–7
    and AIDS 100
    and career women 70
    confessions 92
    and guilt 54
    as masculinizing act 33
    spaces 21, 101
    views of 26, 52–3
AIDS 99–101
    crisis 2, 99
    link with casual sex 88, 99–100
All That Heaven Allows (1955) 39
Andrews, David 58, 59, 90–1,
    127nn5, 6
Ansen, David 45–6
Archer, Anne 7
Atlantic Monthly 112
audiences 59–60, 76, 78, 85, 93, 114,
    126n14
    anticipation 59
    bias 114, 120

condemnation of characters 2, 38,
    81–2, 123n2, 124n1
    double standards 75, 88, 90
    manipulation 21, 37–8, 53–4, 58,
    84, 88, 90–1, 93
    participation 47, 48, 59–60
    questions posed 4, 42
    reactions 1, 2, 38, 42, 68, 85, 93
    sympathy for characters 39–40, 76,
    80, 85, 114
    test 63, 82, 84
    viewpoint 8, 13, 22, 32, 37–8, 42,
    48, 64, 67, 93
    voyeurism 93

Babener, Liahna 69, 72
Baby Boom (1987) 80, 81
Basic Instinct (1992) 51, 78, 79
Belkin, Lisa 117
Berland, Elaine 73
The Big Chill (1983) 126
birth control 95, 96, 97
Black Monday, 1987 70
Bork, Robert 98
bourgeois society 49–50, 101–4
    see also family; home life
Breakfast at Tiffany's 110
break-ins 21, 23–4, 56–7, 122n9

The Bridges of Madison County (1995) 39

Bridget Jones's Diary (2001) 108, 110, 113

Broadcast News (1987) 80, 128n3

Bromley, Susan 62

Bullock, Sandra 114

"bunny boiler" *see under Fatal Attraction*

Bushnell, Candace 110

capitalist identities 102–5

career women 2–3, 39, 55, 56, 62–86, 109–12

    conflict with married women 116–17

    independence 63, 67, 80, 110

    lack of domestic opportunities 64, 65, 94, 109–11, 112

    single 62, 66, 108–20

    threat to men 70–1

    unfulfilled 70, 71, 109

    see also feminism

castration anxiety 47–8, 57, 74, 87

children 90, 127n6

    see also under Fatal Attraction

cinema of attractions 60

cinema audiences *see* audiences

cinema history *see* film history

Close, Glenn 4, 123n2, 126n15

    as Alex Forrest 2, 80, 110, 126n10

Conlon, James 40, 44, 50

contraception *see* birth control

Copjec, Joan 56

core values *see* traditional values

Cowie, Elizabeth 57

Creed, Barbara 46, 47–8

Crystal, Billy 122n12

cultural anxieties 1–2, 55–6, 61, 62, 69, 70, 86

Damages (2007) 126n11

Damico, James 51–2

Dangerous Liaisons (1988) 126n11

Dearden, James 14, 82, 84, 121n4, 125n5

Derry, Charles 59

desire, and death 29, 32, 34

Diabolique (1955) 122n11

Disclosure (1994) 78

Diversion (1979) 14, 125n8

    as inspiration for *Fatal Attraction* 14

divorce 70, 101

Doane, Mary Ann 26, 38

Donahue, Phil 87

Double Indemnity (1944) 53, 126n12

Douglas, Mary 21

Douglas, Michael 1, 51, 53, 63, 71, 75–6, 77–80, 126n11

Dow, Bonnie 115, 119

Durbin, Karen 97, 125n7

Eastwood, Clint 122n1

Eisner, Michael 125n8

Elsaesser, Thomas 39–40, 45

eroticism 28, 87–8, 94

erotic thriller *see under* thriller genres

Falling Down (1993) 78

Faludi, Susan 65, 70–1, 121n2

family

    breakdown 70

    and conflict 34, 42–3, 44

    ideal 45, 64, 98

    law 53, 128n10

    life *see* home life

    photographs 44–5, 121n5

    as repository for morality 64

    resilience 44, 45, 123n4

    triumph of 45, 59, 85

    see also home life; work–life balance

"family values" *see* traditional values
Fatal Attraction (1987)
  adultery *see* adultery
  anti-feminism 62, 70, 71–5: *see also*
    feminism; postfeminist era
  audiences *see* audiences
  blood 13, 31, 32, 46–7
  break-ins *see* break-ins
  and *Bridget Jones's Diary* 108, 110
  "bunny boiler" scene 2, 3, 5, 7,
    23–4, 26, 67
  characters 1–2
  controversy over 2–3, 61, 62
  cynicism 106
  as deterrent to infidelity 1, 4–5, 44,
    62, 87, 107
  director's commentary 10
  endings 82–6
  as film noir 11, 34, 51–8, 124n11
  gross earnings 1
  homage to *Psycho* 8, 30–1, 122n12
  as horror film 45–51
  hybrid genre 4, 61
  iconic status 2, 3, 7, 30
  key motifs 4, 24, 33
  as melodrama 35–45
  as morality tale 2, 4, 20, 87–107
  narrative cues 6–7, 22
  online fan sites 4
  as origin text 3
  Oscar nominations 1
  parodied 3
  plotline 1–33
  popularity 1, 61
  promotion 1, 10
  role of children 8, 9, 10, 11–12, 24–5,
    26–8, 29, 40, 41, 44, 45, 57, 60, 68
  role of telephone 6–7, 14–21, 36,
    122n7
  roller coaster scene 26, 27–8, 60

  sex scenes 1, 28, 29, 59–60, 70, 91
  sexuality 1, 2, 4, 33, 106–7
  technical devices 7, 22, 23–4, 25–6,
    27, 28, 32, 43, 54, 68, 73
  use of color 8–13, 54, 73, 121n3
  violence 1, 40, 57, 59, 66, 124n13
  water 28–33
  and windows 7–8, 38–9, 43, 123n3
  see also film genres
female identities 85, 108–20
  polarization 117–19
feminine desires 74–5, 108
  biological clock 66, 69, 108, 109,
    115–16, 125n3
The Feminine Mystique (Friedan) 69
feminism 2, 3, 55–6
  and anger 113, 115, 125n7
  backlash 2, 65, 80, 81
  debates 4, 61, 62, 107, 109, 117–20
  and *Fatal Attraction* 62–86
  hostility to 63, 64
  targeting men 71
  see also postfeminist era
femme fatale
  calm 57–8
  compared to horror monster 56
  masculinized 55
  psychology of 124n13
  role of 51, 53–4, 56
  sexuality 55
film genres 34–5
  black comedy 78
  classic noir 51, 52, 55–6, 99, 126n12
  erotic thriller *see under* thriller
    genre
  horror *see* horror genre
  melodrama 34, 35–45
  neo-noir 51, 52
  porn 34, 58
  thriller *see* thriller genre

film history 35
film music *see* music
film noir 51–8
Flashdance (1983) 70
Fonda, Jane 114
Forbes magazine 118
Freud, Sigmund 47–8, 89–90
Friday the 13th (1980) 123n5
Friedan, Betty 69

Gavin, John (as Sam, *Psycho*) 8
gender politics 2, 3, 69, 78, 85, 86, 95,
    109
Gledhill, Christine 34
Goimard, Jacques 26
Good Housekeeping 64
The Good Mother (1988) 80
Gottlieb, Lori 112, 128n3
Grant, Barry Keith 123n9
Griffith, Melanie 81

hairstyles 12, 47
The Hand That Rocks the Cradle
    (1992) 125n4
Hanks, Tom 3
Harwood, Sarah 44–5, 47, 124n14
Heigl, Katherine 114
Henricksson, Lisa 88
Hepburn, Audrey 110
Hewitt, Pamela 62
Hirsch, Foster 99
Hitchcock, Alfred, and windows 7–8
Holmlund, Chris 57
home life 8–9, 15, 16, 20–1, 23–4,
    38–9, 40, 101, 122n8
    demands of 40–1
    restrictions of 41–3
    vulnerability 101, 104
horror genre 7, 34, 35, 45–51
    feminist readings 48–9

and illicit sex 48
and monsters 46, 48, 50
Hudson, Kate 114

id, the 49, 50
identity theft 67
Imitation of Life (1935) 39
innocent suffering 26, 50, 51, 77,
    92–3
interior spaces *see* public and private
    spaces
Internet 4

Jaffle, Stanley 85
Jagged Edge (1985) 126n10
Jermyn, Deborah 50–1
Jewel of the Nile (1985) 78
Jones, Amelia 80
Joshel, Sandra 67
Juno (2007) 127n8

Kael, Pauline 46, 74
Keaton, Diane 80
Keesey, Douglas 34, 47
Knocked Up (2007) 127n8
Koch, Ed 127n2
Krutnik, Frank 53, 55

Lansing, Sherry 14, 85, 123n2
Larson, Janet Karsten 105, 113
Latzen, Ellen Hamilton 7
Leigh, Janet 8
Letter from an Unknown Woman
    (1948) 39
Lilith, comparison with Alex
    Forrest 125n7
Longfellow, Henry Wadsworth, "The
    Courtship of Miles Standish" 43
Lyne, Adrian 2, 10, 70–1, 76, 83, 84,
    85, 87, 121n3, 124n1, 125n9

MacMurray, Fred 53
McRobbie, Angela 96–7, 110
Madame Butterfly (Puccini) 36–7, 67–8, 83–4
male passivity 43–4, 57, 74, 77, 85
Manhattan, New York City 52, 128n2
Marcus, Daniel 64
marriage 4, 8, 33, 102
  age at 65–6
  and carnal repression 42, 49, 106
  and happiness 68–9
  panic 109–12, 113
  responsibilities of 5, 17, 77, 102
  and sexuality 49
  see also adultery; home life
Medusa 47
  psychoanalytical explanations 47–8
melodrama *see under* film genres
Mercer, John 44
Merck, Mandy 89
monogamy *see* marriage
Monster-in-Law (2005) 114
monstrous-feminine, the 47–8, 50
Movies That Shook the World (AMC TV) 125n6
Mulvey, Laura 2
  "Visual Pleasure and Narrative Cinema" 2
music, and melodrama 36–7

Naremore, James 51
National Review 76
The Natural (1985) 126n10
Negra, Diane 113
New Right 64
New York City 7, 52, 127n2
New York Times 112, 117
The New Yorker 126n14
Newsweek 46, 63, 65, 66, 111–12, 125n2

Nightmare on Elm Street (1984) 123n5
Nowell-Smith, Geoffrey 35
nudity 8

O'Donnell, Rosie 111
opera 36–7

People's Weekly 87
Phoenix, Arizona 8
phone terror *see under* telephone
Play Misty for Me (1971) 122–3n1
Playland Park, New York 27
police force 74, 83, 106, 127n5
postfeminist era 3, 85–6, 94, 96, 108, 113–14
  heroines 113–16
  impact of *Fatal Attraction* 4, 108–16
  female identities 108–20
  "opt-out revolution" 117
  paradigms 108–9, 116–17
pregnancy 95–9, 104
  and age 116
  and birth control 95, 96
  and casual sex 88
  and entrapment 43, 71, 95
  and falsehood 56–7, 127–8n9
  mental/physical effects 38–9, 45–6
  and miscarriage 96
  and rabbits 122n10
  and rejection 40, 48
  termination *see* abortion
  unplanned 2, 88, 96–7
Presumed Innocent (1990) 80, 81
Psycho (1960) 8, 30–1, 122n12
psychological factors 47–8, 123nn6, 7, 124n15
public and private spaces 42, 50, 102–4
Puccini, Giacomo *see Madame Butterfly*

Rabbit Test (1978) 122n10
rabbits
    associations with fertility 122n10
    in *Fatal Attraction* 2, 3, 5, 7, 23–4,
        26, 30, 66, 67
    pregnancy test 122n10
Reagan era 2, 53, 64, 69, 88, 98
Reagan, Ronald 125n6
Rear Window (1954) 8, 127n7
Rebecca (1940) 125n2
rejection 16–18, 20–1, 38–9, 40, 48
    and revenge 40, 72–3, 79
repression, surplus 42, 49–50
Repulsion (1965) 123n5
revenge 40, 57, 64
Rolling Stone magazine 88
Romancing the Stone (1984) 78
Ronnel, Avital 18
Ryan, Meg 111

Sargent, Lydia 62, 66
seduction
    and danger 58–61, 89, 93, 94, 127n2
    see also sex
Segal, Naomi 31, 73–4
sex
    as crime 53, 56, 58
    and danger 59, 87–8, 89–90, 93–4,
        99–100, 127nn2, 4
    and destruction 29
    drive linked to death drive 29, 32
    and suicide 29, 77, 92
    see also marriage; sexual energy;
        traditional values
Sex and the City (TV series) 113, 128n2
Sex in the City (Bushnell) 110
sexual energy 49
sexual liberation 63, 94–6
sexual perversions 88, 89–90
Shadow of Doubt (1943) 8

The Shield (2004–5) 126n11
Shingler, John 44
Simon, John 76
Single White Female (1992)
    125n4
single women 62, 66, 68, 69, 108–20
    biological clock 66, 69, 108, 109,
        115–16
    and blame 75
    loneliness 66, 126n10
    media portrayals 108–14, 125n4
    and pregnancy 98: *see also*
        pregnancy
    psychosis 66–7, 71–2, 115
    see also career women; marriage
Sirk, Douglas 45
Sleepless in Seattle (1993) 3–4, 111, 112
Stella Dallas (1937) 39
stereotypes 63, 64–5
Stone, Laurie 66

Tanner, Tony 20
Taubin, Amy 2, 128n1
telephone communication 14–21
    phone terror 14, 36, 121n4
    role in *Fatal Attraction* 6–7, 14–21,
        36
    technology 17
Telotte, J. P. 17, 36
Thompson, Joyce 77, 84, 125n8
thriller genres 7
    erotic 34, 58–61, 99, 124n15
traditional values 1, 3, 4–5, 64, 69, 96,
    98, 123n8, 127n8
    assault on 70
Traffic (2000) 79

unemployment 69
upward mobility 101–7
U.S. Census Bureau 64–5

Vavrus, Mary Douglas 117
Vertigo (1958) 127n7
Village Voice 2

Waitress (2007) 127n8
Wall Street (1987) 78
Walters, Barbara 123n2
War of the Roses (1989) 78
Weaver, Sigourney 81
Wechter, Marilyn 73
welfare mothers 98
Westchester, New York State 52
Westerlund-Shands, Kerstin 29
Williams, Linda 60
Williams, Linda Ruth 34, 53, 58, 59,
    79, 123n7, 124n15

Williamson, Judith 45, 100, 123n6
Willis, Ellen 73, 123n4
Winfrey, Oprah 87
Witherspoon, Reese 114
Wood, Robin 49, 127n3
Working Girl (1988) 80, 81
"work–life balance" 108–9, 110, 116,
    117
working women 68, 69–70, 75, 81,
    108–9, 118
    and marriage/motherhood 117–19
    see also career women
The World According to Garp
    (1982) 126n10

Zellweger, Renée 108